THE
Traditional Culture OF
Sussex
BOTH SIDES
OF THE DOWNS

GEOFF DOEL

FONTHILL

*To my dear wife Fran, my fellow researcher,
with thanks for all her support and encouragement.*

Cover illustration: 'Home to the Fold', Clement Lambert. (*Brighton and Hove Museums*)

Fonthill Media Limited
Stroud House
Russell Street
Stroud GL5 3AN

www.fonthillmedia.com
office@fonthillmedia.com

First published in the United Kingdom 2020

British Library Cataloguing in Publication Data:
A catalogue record for this book is available from the British Library

Typeset in 10pt on 13pt Sabon
Printed and bound in England

Acknowledgements

My wife Fran for writing the chapter on Hermits and Anchorites and Hermits, supplying much information on other chapters and for discussions and encouragement and shared visits to the sites.

My parents, grandparents and sister, Sylvia Peters, for much Brighton and Hove 'lore'.

Alan Sutton, the editor, for helpful advice and suggestions.

Sandra Collins, assistant keeper of the Fishermens' Museum, Hastings for information on Christmas customs of the Hastings fishermen.

The Bexhill Museum for permission to use their photo of beating of the bounds at Bexhill, 1925.

The *Petworth Magazine* for permission to use their photo of the Duncton wassailers.

To Jacqueline Simpson and Esme Evans, Librarian of the Sussex Archaeological Society, for information on the Lyminster Dragon lore.

To Janet Pennnington for valuable insights into St Cuthman.

Valmai Goodyear for information on the Lewes Saturday Folk Club and for keeping me informed of Lewes folk events since my move to faraway Canterbury!

Will Duke, John Morgan, Mick Lynn and Liz Randall and the Tonbridge Mummers and Hooideners for joining in many enjoyable and entertaining musical talks/lectures on Sussex traditions and mumming performances and for providing many illuminating insights and superb singing and playing of Sussex songs.

The late lamented Tony Wales for past permission to use photos and information from his stimulating books on Sussex folklore.

Chanctonbury Morris (Dave & Jan Green) & Ditchling Morris (John & Ann Bacon) for inspirational dancing and mumming.

Absent friends: Bob Copper, Ron Spicer, Tony Deane, George Wagstaff, Sandra Goddard and Chris Addison, for very helpful discussions, information, songs and recordings.

Other thanks for use of illustrations: Lewes Castle Museum and the Sussex Archaeological Society, Stonyhurst College, Battle Bonfire Boys, The John Harvey Tap, 'Social Bonfire', 'The Victorian Web, the Regency Society, The Reading Museum of Rural Life, Alan Sutton & Christine Duke.

And, of course, to the inspirational effect of Harvey's Beer!

'The Sheepwash' (above) and 'Landscape with Rainbow and Sheep' (below), both by Clement Lambert. (*Royal Pavilion & Museums, Brighton & Hove*)

Contents

The last team of oxen ploughing in Sussex.

Introduction

This book about Sussex traditional culture explores its organic connection to the landscape and Sussex communities and the links to traditional modes of labour, such as shepherding and fishing. I have been aided and influenced by a number of earlier writers and researchers who have served Sussex well. Arthur Beckett explored folk tales and saints' lore and Mummers plays. Barclay Wills wrote knowingly and movingly on the life of the South Down shepherds. Jacqueline Simpson produced an acclaimed book in the Batsford County folklore series in 1973 (slightly updated in 2002), in turn drawing extensively on Charlotte Latham's *Some West Sussex Superstitions Lingering in 1868* for lore, witchcraft and oral tales. Tony Wales has been an especial inspiration through many excellent books on Sussex lore, customs and song. Chris Hare's 2016 study on *The Secret Shore*, as well as covering smuggling in West Sussex and Hampshire, also helpfully makes good use of Charlotte Latham (whose work is not generally accessible). And there have been a host of folk song collectors in the county to draw attention to the fine songs and singers, one of whom, Bob Copper, wrote several fine books on Sussex life illustrated by songs.

Creative writers, too, have been inspired by Sussex. As early as 1787, Charlotte Smith personified the atmospheric Downs as:

> *... cold and hollow, the inconstant breeze*
> *Sobs thro' the falling leaves and wither'd fern*
> *O'er the tall brow of yonder chalky bourn*
> *The evening shades their gather'd darkness fling,*
> *While by the lingering light I scarce discern*
> *The shrieking night-jar sail on heavy wing.*

And after early years in India Rudyard Kipling found his spiritual home in Sussex:

> *I'm just in love with all these three,*
> *The Weald an' the Marsh an' the Down countrie;*
> *Nor I don't know which I love the most,*
> *The Weald or the Marsh or the white chalk coast!*

... I've given my soul to the Southdown grass,
An' sheep-bells tinkled where you pass.
Oh, Firle an' Ditchling an' sail at sea,
I reckon you keep my soul for me!

There is something very spiritual about the Sussex landscape, recognised by Hilaire Belloc and by Sheila Kaye Smith who set biblical stories in the Sussex landscape in her *Sussex Saints*; just as Duncan Grant and Vanessa Bell set the birth of Christ in a Sussex scene with Sussex shepherds and sheep crooks, Southdown sheep, a trug basket and Downs in the background in their mural in Berwick church.

But there is also a pragmatic dogmatism and subtle stubbornness in the Sussex character, caught in Victor Cook's Sussex dialect poem 'Sussex Won't Be Druv'

But them as comes to Sussex,
They mustn't push and shove,
For Sussex will be Sussex,
And Sussex won't be druv!

Mus Wilfred come to Sussex,
Us heaved a stone at he,
Because he reckoned he could teach
Our Sussex fishers how to reach
The fishes in the sea.

But when he dwelt among us,
Us gave un land and luv,
For Sussex will be Sussex,
And Sussex won't be druv!

... There ant no place like Sussex
Until ye goos above,
But Sussex will be Sussex,
And Sussex won't be druv!

And then there is the humour and fatalism of Stella Gibbons' *Cold Comfort Farm*. So what is there left to write about? Well, the general folklore books on Sussex have not really explored the reasons behind the Bonfire traditions and their conflicts and controversies. Neither has the fascinating subject of Sussex tipteering been fully explored geographically and textually. There are many experts on Sussex folksong, but again the general studies have tended to omit the subject. Tony Wales is very strong on seasonal customs, but there is a case for bringing all this together in one study. Also I have visited many of the customs and there is new research on them, as well as on legends in the past 30 or 40 years which needs to be incorporated in a new study.

I was brought up in Hove and the reader will detect a certain bias towards Brighton, Hove and Lewes (a favourite place). But as Arthur Beckett, Jacqueline Simpson, Tony Wales and

Nativity Scene Berwick Church Murals

Haymaking Near Amberley.

Chris Hare are strong on West Sussex I am hoping my bias may be a useful corrective. The title also shows my primary love of the Downland and how it slopes to the south the coast, with the steep scarp slope northwards to the Weald with changing habitats.

Parts of this book draw on the Sussex sections of two small studies from the very useful Meresborough Press series of local books, sponsored by South East Arts, which I wrote with my wife Fran and the late Tony Deane on midwinter traditions and on spring and summer customs. Fran has supplied the whole of the chapter in the present book on hermits and anchorites, a favourite topic of hers, and she has also supplied some of the saints' lore.

We moved, because of work to Kent, currently at Canterbury, but I still have family in Sussex and give talks there and visit the county as often as I can, because it draws like a magnet. To leave the last word with Rudyard Kipling, from his poem 'Sussex', which ingeniously links sheep and ships:

> *Here leaps ashore the full Sou'west*
> *All heavy-winged with brine,*
> *Here lies above the folded crest*
> *The Channel's leaden line*
> *And here the sea-fogs lap and cling,*
> *And here, each warning each,*
> *The sheep-bells and the ship-bells ring*
> *Along the hidden beach.*

Geoff Doel, Canterbury

1
Legends in the Landscape

The people of Sussex endowed their surroundings with a rich mystery of associations—stories of the origins of physical sites, strange monsters and heroes, ancient battles and the miracles of saints. In Sussex, dragon and devil-lore are peculiarly prevalent, and the *Anglo-Saxon Chronicle* refers to serpents being sited in Sussex.

The Lyminster Dragon

One Anglo-Saxon word for dragon is 'nicor' and the dragon legends at Lyminster involving a dragon in the Knucker Hole are therefore highly likely to go back to Anglo-Saxon times, especially as the oldest tradition invokes a 'King of Sussex'. Sussex ceased to be an independent kingdom at the end of the seventh century, although there were client kings, owing allegiance to the kingdom of Wessex after that. There was an Anglo Saxon Benedictine nunnery at Lyminster which may have recorded and preserved traditions. This was the nunnery from which Sweyn, the youngest son of Godwin, earl of Kent, abducted Edgwina, for which he was banished the kingdom with fatal results for the Anglo-Saxon royal family, as he encouraged the king of Norway, Harald Hardraga, to invade England. Although Harold Godwin defeated Hardraga a few days before he lost at Hastings, it seems very likely that without the Hardraga/Sweyn diversion, Harold would have had enough unexhausted troops to defeat William of Normandy.

There is a singular pool near Lyminster Church called the Knucker Hole described by Horsfield in 1835:

> Near the church is a pond, about 60 feet in diameter, and 20 feet deep, supplied from a never-failing spring at the bottom. It is the most copious spring on the south side of the Downs, and is called the Knucker-hole.

The earliest tale is of a wandering knight who killed a dragon which was exacting tribute of young people from the kingdom for its food. The knight saved the king of Sussex's daughter and in some versions married her, but in others succumbed to the dragon's poisonous breath

Above left: The Knucker Hole, Lyminster, *c.* 1866.

Above right: Lyminster font and dragon slater's tomb. (*Geoff Doel*)

and died along with the dragon. His gravestone, known as 'The Slayer's Stone', was pointed out in Lyminster churchyard and has now been moved inside the church. Jacqueline Simpson records traditions that local children used to say that the ridges on the stone (formed by rain) were made by the dragon trying to get at the body of his slayer; also that an old man used to sell bottles of water from the pool as a cure for ailments. There were watercress beds and the librarian of the Sussex Archaeological Society, Esme Evans has found evidence of these marked on a 6 inch OS map of 1914. A small stream drains away westwards to the Arun. The beds were cleared, deepened, and stocked with fish, presumably why they are fenced off.

There are versions of the story in Samuel Evershed's 'Legend of the Dragon-Slayer of Lyminster' and in Arthur Beckett's 'The Wonderful Weald'. Knights and a miller die in the attempt to kill the dragon and win the princess and a local lad who has been fighting abroad returns home and kills the dragon and marries the princess. A version from a Lyminster hedger, printed in the *Sussex County Magazine* in 1929, named a ploughman Jim Puttock as the dragon slayer. Other variants call him Jim Pulk and say that he kills the dragon by trickery such as a poisoned Sussex pie or suet pudding (the dragon swallowed cart, horse and pie). In some versions the hero dies whilst celebrating at a local pub, killed by the after effect of fumes. One variant has a knight surviving and nursed back to health by the princess. Versions from teams of Morris dancers in the late twentieth century blame the hero's death on the brand of beer consumed (no longer in production)!

One account has the dragon shaped half like a serpent and half like a woman. Moreover, it had wings, and its habit was to swoop down on the farmers' cattle and unsuspecting people and carry them off to its home in the marshes and devour them there.

St Leonard's Forest Dragons

St Leonard's Forest also has dragon traditions. The saint had no historical connection with Sussex, but local tradition records St Leonard living as a hermit in the forest, where he slew a dragon who was threatening Horsham, lilies of the valley springing up where drops of his (or in some version the dragon's) blood fell. The George & Dragon pub at Dragon's Green at the edge of the Forest is incorrectly named, as the dragon-slaying saint here should be St Leonard.

St Leonard's victory was supposed to rid the forest of snakes, but in 1614, John Trundle published an account, based on interviews with four local people who claimed to have seen a dragon in the forest:

> True and Wonderful. A Discourse relating a strange and monstrous Serpent (or Dragon) lately discovered, and yet living, to the great Annoyance and divers Slaughters both of Men and Cattell, by his strong and violent Poyson. In Sussex, two miles from Horsham, in a Woode called St Leonard's Forest, and thirtie Miles from London, this present month of August, 1614. With the true Generation of Serpents.
>
> In Sussex, there is a pretty market-towne, called Horsham, neare unto it a forrest called St Leonard's Forrest, and there, in a vast and unfrequented place, heathie, vaultie, full of unwholesome shades and overgrown hollowes, where this serpent is thought to be bred; but, wheresoever bred, certaine and too true it is, that there it yet lives. Within three or four miles compasse, are its usual haunts, often-times at a place called Faygate, and it hath been seene within halfe a mile of Horsham; a wonder, no doubt, most terrible and noisome to the inhabitants thereabouts. There is always in his tracke or path left a glutinous and slimie matter (as by a small similitude we may perceive in a snail's) which is very corrupt and offensive to the scent; insomuch that they perceive the air to be putrified withal, which must needes be very dangerous. For though the corruption of it cannot strike the outward part of a man, unless heated into his blood; yet by receiving it in at any of our breathing organs (the mouth or nose) it is by authorities of all authors, writing in that kinde, mortall and deadlie.
>
> This serpent (or dragon, as some call it) is reputed to be nine feete, or rather more, in length, and shaped almost in the form of an axletree of a cart; a quantitie of thickness in the middest, and somewhat smaller at both ends. The former part, which he shootes forth as a necke, is supposed to be an elle long; with a white ring, as it were, of scales about it. The scales along his backe seem to be blackish, and so much as is discovered under his bellie, appeareth to be red.
>
> It is likewise discovered to have large feete, but the eye may be deceived; for some suppose that serpents have no feete, but glide upon certain ribbes and scales, which both defend them from the upper part of their throat unto the lower part of their bellie, and also cause them to move much faster. For so this doth, and rids way as fast as a man can run. He is of countenance very proud, and at the sight or hearing of men or cattel, will raise his necke upright, and seem to listen and look about, with great arrogancy. There are likewise on either side of him discovered two great bunches so big as a large footeball, and (as some thinke) will in time grow to wings; but God, I hope, will (to defend the poor people in the neighbourhood) that he shall be destroyed before he grow so fledge.
>
> He will cast his venome about four rodde from him, as by woeful experience it was proved on the bodies of a man and woman coming that way, who afterwards were found dead, being

poisoned and very much swelled, but not prayed upon. Likewise a man going to chase it and, as he imagined, to destroy it with two mastive dogs, as yet not knowing the great danger of it, his dogs were both killed, and he himself glad to return with haste to preserve his own life. Yet this is to be noted, that the dogs were not prayed upon, but slaine and left whole; for his food is thought to be, for the most part, in a conie-warren, which he much frequents; and it is found much scanted and impaired in the increase it had woont to afford.

The persons, whose names are hereunder printed, have seene this serpent, besides divers others, as the carrier of Horsam, who lieth at the White Horse in Souhwark, and who can certifie the truth of all that has been here related.

John Steele

Christopher Holder

And a Widow Woman dwelling neare Faygate.

A dragon is said to have curled itself around Bignor Hill. And, according to Charlotte Latham's pamphlet of 1867 on 'West Sussex Superstitions', the village of Fittleworth was terrorized by 'an audacious large snake'. At Offington serpents were said to guard treasure in an underground tunnel under Cissbury Ring, this being a mythical and traditional Viking and Anglo-Saxon link between dragons and treasure, as in the poem *Beowulf*.

The Devil

The countryman was always reluctant to name the Devil. The Reverend W. D. Parish gives an example of this in connection with the golden calf legend at Clayton:

> In the Downs there's a golden calf buried; people know very well where it is and could show you. Any day.
> 'Then why don't you dig it up?'
> 'Oh, it's not allowed; *he* wouldn't let them.'
> 'Has anyone ever tried?'
> 'Oh yes, but it's never there when you look; *he* moves it away.'

Traditions of the Devil trying to prevent the construction of churches are frequent in Sussex, with a curious compromise negotiated at Hollington, near the edge of Hastings, which is said to explain its church's original isolation and woodland setting. The Devil thwarted continual attempts to build the church on a more populous site and eventually offered to stop his disruption if he could be allowed to select the site, which he did in a remote spot, surrounding it with a wood to increase its isolation to deter worshippers!

There are natural and man-made features called devil's dykes all over the south and west of England, several of which can be shown by charters to be originally named after the Anglo-Saxon god Woden, with names such as the Wansdyke. These massive features, some of which have defensive ditches, (or look as if they have) were named after the Anglo-Saxon god of war; the early Christian missionaries were encouraged by the Papacy to link pagan gods to the Devil, hence the renaming.

The Devil's Dyke.

Sussex has a particularly famous devil's dyke, near Hangleton on the Downs with a superb legend attached which was strongly surviving in the oral tradition in my boyhood in Hove. I heard versions from my parents, grandparents, teachers and cub mistresses. The earliest traceable name for the Sussex devil's dyke is 'Poor Man's Walls'—'poor man' being another Sussex way of avoiding naming the Devil directly. Two mounds at the north of the dyke are called the devil's grave and the devil's wife's grave. The legend concerning this devil's dyke is that the Devil, provoked by the conversion of Sussex and the building of numerous churches in the Weald, determined to cut a dyke in a single night through the Downs to flood the Weald with sea water and engulf the new churches. The earliest version I have so far traced of this legends is told in Thomas Horsfield's *The History and Antiquities and Topography of Sussex* of 1835, quoted from another early nineteenth century writer, William Shoburl. This version, interestingly, follows the Sussex (and elsewhere) tradition of not specifically naming the Devil, but using alternatives such 'The Poor Man', which suggests it is a version taken down from a local account:

Poor Man's Wall, now Devil's Dyke

It is ascribed (says Mr. Shoburl) to the grand author of evil, who beholding with envy the numerous churches of the weald, determined to form a channel which should admit the sea, and thus inundate that whole tract, with its pious inhabitants. This plan, as we are further told, was disconcerted by an old woman, who being roused from her midnight slumbers by the noise which the progress of the work occasioned, peeped out of her chamber window, and had no difficulty to recognise the infernal agent. She perceived likewise the object of his undertaking, and with admirable presence of mind, held a burning candle from the casement. The mischievous spirit mistaking the light for the rising sun, was so scared, that he instantly quitted his unfinished work, and made a hasty retreat.

William Axon tells a very similar story in his 1897 *Bygone Sussex*, adding that 'The medieval devil could only do his malicious deeds in the dark'. Other versions say that the Devil started digging at Poynings and was only allowed one night to complete the task. Spadefulls of earth became local landmarks such as Chanctonbury and Cissbury Rings and Mount Caburn and

that he was thwarted by a nun lighting a candle and causing the cock to crow early. In Harrison Ainsworth's melodramatic novel *Ovingdean Grange*, St Cuthman and Sister Ursula conspire to thwart the Devil, whilst Hilaire Belloc invokes St Dunstan in *The Four Men* (1912).

In his anger at leaving his work uncompleted, the Devil hurled or kicked the Goldstone, an unusual stone that glinted with quartz, once thought to be a meteorite, but more likely a sarsen stone or breccia, to Goldstone Bottom. An article, 'The Goldstone, Hove Park', by H. S. Toms in 1932 shows that the area had been open downland and that the stone stood on the western of the valley, not far south of the Shoreham road on land farmed by Farmer Rigden of Goldstone Farm. Interest in the stone and its legends attracted visitors to the annoyance of William Rigden, who was concerned about damage to his crops and paid two labourers to dig a pit near Goldstone Barn and drag the stone to it and bury it in 1834. It had just been buried when Thomas Horsfield wrote his book on Sussex and he describes the stone and attacks its burial:

Goldstone Bottom

It received its name from a large stone there situated, called Goldstone. It is supposed by many to be the 'Gorsed', or sacred stone, of the ancient Britons. It was one of the largest and most remarkable of the Druidical stones upon the Downs. It was situated in the southern entrance to the retired valley, which runs up behind the church of Hove. It was between six and seven feet in height, and its impressive size and remarkable outlines gave to it an aspect which spake of its antiquity, and its mysterious and sacred character. This very interesting remain, about a year since, at great expense of labour, was removed from its situation and thrown into a deep excavation made by its side to receive it. It is hardly possible to believe that the value of the small spot of ground it occupied could have led to this unfeeling sacrilege, or that any utilitarian considerations could have induced its removal; for the value of landed property is certainly not improved, to educated and enlightened minds, by removing from it so curious a memorial of its possession and occupation by the earliest inhabitants of our isle... North of this stone, there are, or lately were, at the extremity of the valley, the remains of what has been deemed a Druidical circle of stones.

'Druids' Stone' (Goldstone), New Park, Hove, 1925.

In the eighteenth century William Stukeley referred to a 'grey weather' stone in the area and there is a reference to twenty stones labelled 'Tolman' or 'Holy Stone of the Druids'. These eighteenth and early nineteenth century references to the druids and druidical stones are typical of the confusion between the cultures of the late Stone Age and the Bronze Age (to which stone circles and tumuli belong) and the later Iron Age and Celtic cultures which featured druidism. Two drawings of the stones survive, one showing sixteen stones including a segment of a circle, and the other six stones. There is a later reference to the stones in a letter from Rev J. Douglas to the geologist Gideon Mantell in 1818, which says that near to the Goldstone 'is a dilapidated cirque, composed of large stones of the same kind'.

 The stones were cleared in the 1840s and there are traditions that some of the smaller stones were placed at the base of the Victoria Fountain, erected in the Old Steine in 1846. The larger stones were thought to be either buried or used to fill in the old pond in Goldstone Bottom. In 1900 it is said that only one man (a boy at the time-possibly later a verger of St Andrew's Church, Hove called Mr Comford) remembered where the stone was buried. It was dug up in 1900 and there is a surviving photograph of this event. It was set up in Hove Park in 1906, where it still remains. The Brighton and Hove Albion Football Club for many years played at the nearby Goldstone Ground, with jokes about the Devil's skills at football, when kicking the stone!

 The Devil is said to be able to be raised by running seven times around Chanctonbury Ring, when he will offer you a bowl of soup! The Devil's Jumps, five large bell barrows on Treyford Hill—the best preserved bronze age group of barrows in Sussex, has a legend involving the Devil and the Scandinavian god Thor (who was known as Thunor to the Anglo-Saxons and after whom Thursday is named). The Devil disturbed Thor with his jumping and teased him that he was too old to jump, at which provocation Thor hurled a large boulder into the Devil's midriff and the Devil has not been seen there since!

 The Devil's Humps, also known as the Kings Graves, are four Bronze Age barrows situated on Bow Hill on the South Downs near Stoughton. According to the legend, the men of Chichester defeated a Viking war party in the vale and the Viking leaders were buried in the Devil's Humps, giving them their alternative name of The Kings' Graves. Many of the Viking dead lie where they

Digging up the Goldstone,
1900.

fell, under the yew trees on the slopes of the hill. Their ghosts are said to haunt the yew groves, and the trees themselves are said to come alive at night. The origin of this tale might be the defeat of the Danes in 894. According to the *Anglo-Saxon Chronicle*, when the host that had besieged Exeter sailed back on its way home, it harried inland in Sussex near Chichester, but the garrison put them to flight and slew many hundred of them, capturing some of their ships.

There is a Devil's Bog in the Ashdown Forest, near the Roman road, Stane Street, a section of which is known as The Devil's Road. There is a Devil's Book or Brook near Mount Caburn and a six mile Devil's Ditch running from near Halnaker to near West Stoke. There was a Devil's Chimney off Beachy Head, but that has collapsed. According to Cecile Woodford:

> Sussex countryfolk believe you will be unlucky if you eat or pick blackberries after 10th October; for during the night the Devil goes around spitting on all the bushes—so marking the fruit for himself … Beware, too, if you go a'nutting on a Sunday because the Devil will hold the branches down for you—out of sheer appreciation of your breaking the Sabbath.

St Dunstan & the Devil

St Dunstan (924-988) was an expert jeweller and smith and he continued to practise these skills during his twenty-eight years as archbishop of Canterbury. One of the best loved stories about him (traceable to a twelfth century life by Eadmer), is how the Devil tried to seduce him in the guise of a lady whilst working at his anvil in Mayfield and how he tweaked the

St Dunstan and the Devil—*c.* 15th century chausuble. (*Stonyhurst College*)

Devil's nose with his red hot tongs. The Devil flew through the roof with St Dunstan still holding on to his nose and they fell to earth at St Dunstan's Bridge by a well near Tonbridge, into which the Devil dipped his nose, turning it to the chalybeate well which caused the foundation of Tunbridge Wells and explains the terrible taste of the Tunbridge Wells spa water! As one visitor said: 'Tunbridge Wells—of all the villainous hot springs I know there is none of which the sulphur tastes so exceedingly diabolic!'

There is a lively traditional account of this story in Arthur Beckett's *The Wonderful Weald*:

Now Dunstan, being Archbishop of Canterbury, and coming to Mayfield, there founded the first Christian Church for the salvation of the hinds and swineherds who lived in this wild part of Sussex. Whereupon the Devil, not liking the matter, for that he looked upon the men of the neighbouring Weald as his own lawful prey, determined to destroy and wreck the edifice. He appeared to Dunstan at divers times and in many disguises, always seeking to destroy him, but never, by reason of the archbishop's great holiness, so succeeding.

Now Dunstan was not only a holy and learned man, but he had much skill in the working of both gold and iron, and one day while he thus fashioned certain sacred vessels required for the use of the Church and was hammering the red-hot metal at his anvil, the tongs by which he held the iron being hot. Dunstan seized his persecutor by the nose with red-hot tongs, so that his enemy roared lustily with pain. The Devil soared aloft and espied a spring at the place where Tunbridge Wells is built, which lies 8 miles from this very spot. There he came to earth, and thrusting his nose into the bubbling spring still to be found there, he thus cooled it.

> 'Saynt Dunstan, as ye story goes
> Caught old Sathanus by ye nose,
> He tugged soe hard and made hym roar,
> That he was heard 3 miles and more'

Mayfield—ruins of the Archbishop's Palace.

The tongs & anvil are on show at the archbishop's palace at Mayfield. Another encounter between St Dunstan and the Devil at Mayfield explains the lucky associations of horseshoes. When the Devil came to Dunstan's forge the saint nailed a horseshoe to the Devil's cloven hoof and only removed it on condition that he promised never to enter a house on which a horseshoe was hung. Charlotte Latham in her valuable work discusses this tradition:

> If you nail a horseshoe that you have picked up over your door it will prevent all witches and evil spirits crossing the threshold. I have seen several doors that can boast of this protecting talisman.

An amusing folktale where St Dunstan rather surprisingly co-operates with the Devil tells about Dunstan brewing beer to sell and being worried about competition from cider. So he agrees to the Devil creating a frost from 17-19 May each year to blight the apple trees!

Charlotte Latham lists three further pieces of folklore about the Devil. She was told by a farmer's wife at Hying near Arundel of what her charwoman told her about the Devil whilst making blackberry jam):

> Why I thought everybody knows that the Devil went round on the 10th of October, and spat on all the blackberries, and that if any person were to eat one on the eleventh they or some belonging to them would die or fall into great trouble before the year was out.
>
> The watchfulness of the said Evil Spirit makes it dangerous to go out nutting on a Sunday, and worthy mothers may be heard warning children against it by assuring them that, if they did so, the Devil will hold down the branches for them. We have a saying amongst us, 'as black at the Devil's nutting bag', which seems associated with this belief.
>
> The fern-owl (*Strix Camrimolgus*) is in the west of Sussex called the puck-bird, or puck, which was an old Gothic word for Satan; and it probably received the name from a belief existing among the lower class of persons that it is a mischievous sprite, which inflicts on calves and heifers a disease here called the 'puck complaint', and in some parts of England the puckeridge.

Mike Mills & the Devil

One Sussex man became immortal through an encounter and race with the Devil linked to 'Mike Mills' Race', an avenue of trees in St Leonard's Forest. The earliest written account of this that I have traced of this in volume 13 of John Limbird's *The Mirror of Literature*, 1829, where the anecdote quoted is attributed to 'W. Bergen':

> … a beautiful avenue, a mile and a quarter long, containing about 15,000 fully grown trees. There is a legend connected with this 'race', viz that this part of Horsham Forest was the haunt of Mike Mills, a noted smuggler, whom his Satanic Majesty had often endeavored to carry off in vain. He therefore determined on attacking him in his strong hold; and accordingly met Mike one night accompanied by other more congenial spirits, when old Nick challenged Mike as his property. Mike, nothing daunted, set down his tubs, took advantage of Nick's old age, and challenged him to a race. 'If you can catch me, Nick, before I get to the end of the avenue, you shall have me; if

not, you'll have nothing more to do with me.'—'Agreed', says Nick. Away ran Mike—away ran Nick. Nick being of too hot a temperament was soon knocked up, and Mike won the race by half a mile; from which circumstance the place was named, and Mike Mills rendered immortal.

Another version says that Mike ran so fast that some of the trees caught fire! Apparently Mike Mills did exist and arranged for the planting of the avenue in 1722; perhaps he was a wealthy smuggler?

The Sussex Farmer's Old Wife

Arthur Beckett gives the text of this misogynist song about the Devil in his book *The Spirit of the Downs*. It is a brave man who will now sing this at a folk club!:

> *There was an old farmer in Sussex did dwell,*
> *(chorus of whistlers)*
> *And he had a bad wife, as many knew well.*
> *(chorus of whistlers)*
>
> *Then Satan came to the old man at plough.*
> *'One of your family I must have now.*
>
> *It is not your eldest son that I do crave,*
> *But 'tis your old wife, and she I will have'.*
>
> *'O welcome! Good Satan, with all of my heart;*
> *I hope you and she will never more part!'*
>
> *Now Satan he got the old wife on his back,*
> *And he lugged her along like a pedlar's pack.*
>
> *He trudged away till he came to Hell's Gate,*
> *Says he, 'Here take an old Sussex man's mate'.*
>
> *Oh! then she did kick all the young imps about,*
> *Says one to the other, 'Let's try turn her out!*
>
> *She spied seven devils, all dancing in chains,*
> *She's up with her patterns and knocked out their brains.*
>
> *She knocked old Satan against the wall.*
> *'Take her back daddy, she'll murder us all!*
>
> *Now he's bundled her up on his back again,*
> *And to her old husband he's took her again.*

I've been a tormentor the whole of my life,
But I ne'er was tormented till I took your wife!

Which proves that the women is worse than the men,
'Cause they go to Hell and get thrown out again.

Bevis of Hampton

It is said that a prehistoric barrow in Arundel Park is the grave of Bevis of Hampton and that he ended his days as the castle's gatekeeper; he was said to have thrown his sword into the castle park as he was dying, asking that he be buried where the sword landed; the alleged sword is in the castle armory. Bevis Tower was said to have been built to accommodate him and he rode a large horse named 'Hirondelle', which is French for swallow or martin; the county badge for Sussex is the martlet.

There is a fourteenth century romance about Bevis, who was so large that he could wade across to the Isle of Wight. Arthur Beckett's account is:

> Sir Bevis was the giant warder who guarded the gate of the old Arundel Castle (called in 'Le Morte d'Arthur' the 'Castle of Magouns') with his sword Morglory. Bevis's wages as warder of the gate consisted of two weekly hogsheads of beer, an ox and supplies of bread and mustard in proportion. When he required exercise he waded the Channel to the Isle of Wight.

Bevis was also connected to Hampton (Southampton) and when travelling between there and Arundel he used to stop at Bosham to wash his dogs. A huge pole was at one time suspended horizontally inside the nave of Bosham Church and was supposed to be Bevis's staff, which he used to stride across Bosham harbour in one step. On Telegraph Hill at Compton there is a Long Barrow some 210 feet long which is called both Bevis's Thumb and The Devil's Thumb.

Some prehistoric sites in the Sussex landscapes attracted titles concerning legends or traditions that are now lost, such as the circular tumulus on the downs near Alfriston called The Five Lords.

The Long Man of Wilmington

Recent scientific soil analysis suggests that this huge figure outlined on the Downs is late medieval or Tudor. There are descriptions of the figure from 1787 and 1790 and drawings from 1710 and *c.* 1781. Mrs Downs, who was born in 1840 and spent her early years at Wilmington Priory, 'deplored the careless manner in which he had been restored'. She confirmed that he had originally held a scythe and writes that 'the feet of the figure have been altered.' A Local antiquarian, T. C. Woodman, confirms this in a pamphlet of 1900:

> The figure, as many of us can still remember it, was formerly only visible at times … the feet of the figure have been quite altered, now they are sideways, formerly they were foreshortened, and the form was coming straight forward.

But the Long Man has collected a body of folklore, much of it associated with an earlier legendary giant in the area named Gill and collected by J. P. Emslie in the early twentieth century. All versions agree that a giant lived on Windover Hill and that the Long Man figure was either his outline or a memorial. Versions of his death are that a shepherd killed him with his rock-hard bread and cheese, that he fell whilst pursuing a companion female called Eve, whose outline was on the same hill as the modern white horse figure at Litlington, that pilgrims killed him on their way to Wilmington Priory, or that he was killed by a rival giant throwing boulders at him from Firle Beacon.

Cyril Phillips, a traditional musician, singer and story teller who lived on a farm near Lewes, tells of a story collected from a one-armed shepherd who tended his flock on the Downs near the Long Man:

> There were two giants, one on the hill over there, and the other on Mount Caburn about four miles away. They were both flint-crackers, and they used to chat to each other across the valley. One day they fell out, and the Caburn Giant threw his flint hammer and knocked the Long Man out. So they buried him there just where he lay, and you can still see his outline.

This is Cyril Phillips's monologue on the *Long Man*, printed in the magazine of The English Folk Dance and Song Society:

> *Oive lived round ere since the year '21*
> *And during that time, oive had lots of fun.*
> *Oi came from the West Country, where legends are told,*
> *And some of the stories are both daring and bold.*
> *But few can compare with one that I heard,*

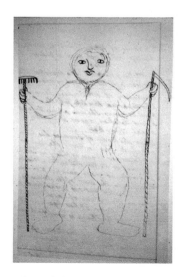 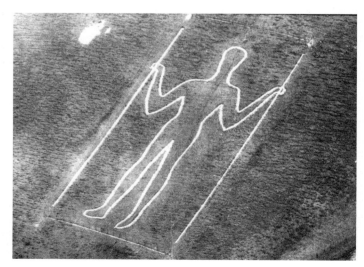

Above left: Long Man of Wilmington. (*William Burrell, Sussex Arch. Society*)

Above right: Long Man of Wilmington—aerial photo, 1918.

From an old timer, a downland shepherd.
Oive had many a chat with these old boys,
Away on the Downs, far from the noise.
The question arose about the Long Man,
He's on the hillside with sticks in his hand.
How did he get there? When did he die?
And this is the story that he told to oi.

In days that are gone, many centuries ago,
There were two mighty Giants, he'd have me to know.
One lived on the Caburn, about four miles away,
The other on Windover, over Wilmington way.
Their job were flint-cracking, that's what he said,
And they smashed flints with hammers as big as your head.
While working away, they both used to shout,
Away cross the valley, there is no doubt.
It was only a chat, but a thunderous roar,
And everyone round there just shook to the core.
There was an argument, one day, he said,
And the Wilmington man yelled 'You ought to be dead.'

Now this riled the Giant on Mount Caburn Hill.
And for quite a while he stood perfectly still.
Then up with his hammer, and took a good aim,
To hit his opponent and just make him lame.
The shot was remarkable for such a long throw,
And being a direct hit was a Jolly Good Show.
Now they buried him there, just where he lay,
You can still see his outline to this very day.
We know he is lying there quite safe and sound—
But what happened to the other one on the Caburn mound?
Where did he come from, where did he go—
Well it's only a legend, so you really don't know.
Perhaps he fell in the sea, from a boat or a raft—
Oi only know one thing—it all sound a bit daft!

There are other memories of Gill in the landscape—a Gills' Lap in the Ashdown Forest and a Gill's Grave on Mount Caburn, from where he is supposed to have hurled his hammer. There is a local weather saying: 'When Firle or Long Man wears a cap/We in the valley (or at A'ston - i.e. Alfriston) gets a drap'.

There was a tradition amongst local shepherds that King Arthur had fought a battle on the Downs very near to the Long Man, possibly at Flossenden.

The Trundle & Aaron's Golden Calf

The Trundle is a Neolithic causewayed enclosure overlooking Goodwood Race Course. Aaron's Golden Calf is said to be buried there, guarded by the Devil, who shifts the location to avoid it being found. Brewer's *Dictionary of Phrase and Fable* (1870) states that 'Aaron's Golden Calf is buried in Rook's Hill, this being the name of the hill as a whole, while the Trundle, strictly speaking, is the hill fort on the summit. No one could dig up the Golden Calf because whenever anyone tried the Devil moved it away'. There is also a similar tradition of a golden calf buried on Clayton Hill and protected by the Devil.

Kingley Vale & the Vikings

Kingley Vale is a splendid grove of yew trees on the South Downs north of Chichester. By tradition it is the site of the burial of Viking leaders slain by local Chichester men in battle in 894. One version mentions gold and other booty gathered by the Viking host guarded by a ghostly calf, which can still be heard bleating as it roams the wooded slopes below the Trundle. On the ridge are a group of Bronze Age barrows called 'The Kings' Graves'.

The Ditchling Hounds

Ditchling Beacon is haunted by a phantom hunt known locally as the Witch Hounds. The cry of the hounds, hoofbeats of horses and a hunting horn can all be heard, but nothing can be seen.

Cowdray House and the Cowdray Curse

Arthur Beckett tells the story:

> When Sir Anthony Browne took possession of Battle Abbey he destroyed the church and lodged himself in the abbot's quarters, where he gave a great feast. In the middle of the festivities there came into the hall one of the dispossessed monks, and holding up his hand he solemnly cursed Sir Anthony, declaring that his family should perish by fire and water. The curse was fulfilled in 1793 when Cowdray was destroyed by fire; and, one week later, the last Viscount Montague, in attempting to shoot certain falls of the river Rhine, was drowned. So perished the last of the noble Montagues.

Two further male members of the family were drowned in 1815.

St Ann's Well, Hove

St Ann's Well's Gardens in Hove, formerly in the Wick Estate, featured a famous chalybeate well which became quite a cult place in the nineteenth century, with an elegant well-house to

The Chalybeate St Anne's Wells Gardens. (*Juvenile Varieties, early c. 19th century*)

take the waters. The well was dedicated to the Virgin's mother St Ann, a shadowy Biblical figure possibly invoked to Christianize a number of wells dedicated to the pagan divinity Anu. In legend the Spring is named after the Lady Annefrieda and marks the spot where her local peasant lover was killed by his rival the Black Knight; Ann's tears caused the spring to flow.

An account of the chalybeate waters at the well exists from 1761 and was frequently quoted): 'The water was soft, not unpleasingly martial and temperate in point of heat. The water looked as though two or three drops of milk had been distilled into it and it was at its most pellucid after dry weather'.

It is shown on a map of 1819 as a 'mineral spring', and was often known as 'the Chalybeate'. Famous people and royalty such as Queen Adelaide and Princess Augusta took the waters there, as did Mrs Fitzherbert, who wrote: 'I certainly was very unwell the first two or three days when I came here but am wonderfully improved both in health and strength. I drink the Chalybeate waters every day, similar to those of Tonbridge'.

The Charleses at Beachy Head

The Charleses were seven masses of chalk which stuck out in front of Beachy Head, and collapsed in 1810. Local weather lore about them said: 'When the Charleses wear a cap, the clouds weep'. They were also known as 'The Churls', because of their angry, threatening look.

2

Legendary and Ghostly Sussex

Christmas Ghost Stories and Hauntings

Christmas is the most prevalent time for hauntings and Sussex in no exception. Traditionally, solsticial times were those when the spirit world was believed to be most clearly connected to the 'real' world and the twelve days of Christmas have been suggested as originating as a gap between the old Julian calendar and even earlier lunar calendars—a crack in time through which spirits could penetrate at this season.

The De Braoses of Bramber

The thirteenth century owner of Bramber Castle, William De Braose occurred the enmity of King John—not a difficult thing to do! De Braose had acquired much land in England, Wales and Ireland and had been a loyal supporter of both Richard I and later John and was favoured by them both. De Braose's wife is said to have made an indiscreet comment that John had murdered his nephew, Prince Arthur (which he probably did), but John may simply have been after the Braose money and lands. John outlawed De Braose, saying that he owed money to the Crown for his estates. De Braose escaped first to Ireland, then to Wales, where he joined up with enemies of the king, and then to France. His lands including Bramber Castle were seized, and his wife, Maud, described by Gerald of Wales as 'a prudent and chaste woman' and eldest son fell into John's hands; they were imprisoned and starved to death. According to tradition Maud and two young children are said to have starved to death in Bramber Castle and the ghosts of the children are sometimes encountered at Christmas time in Bramber, holding their hands out for food. If they are spoken to, the children disappear. There are sometimes said to be four young children, sometimes three—'a boy and two girls, all skin and bones and their clothing in rags, have been seen many times begging for a scrap of food, most frequently in December.'

But, historically, De Braose's wife & son were starved at either Windsor or Corfe and the eldest son was in his twenties. The brutal persecution of the De Braoses shocked the other barons, who rebelled against the king's injustice, leading to Magna Carta, which states: 'No

Bramber Castle. (*engraving by Hollar*)

man shall be taken, imprisoned, outlawed, banished or in any was destroyed, nor will we proceed or prosecute him, except by the lawful judgment of his peers'.

De Braose's younger son eventually regained some of his father's lands, but the family influence declined. Bramber Castle passed by marriage to the Mowbray family after 1337 and it was later owned by the Howards, dukes of Norfolk. The later John de Braose died in a riding accident and a ghostly white horse is seen at night at Bramber Castle, galloping around the moat.

Bramber Castle is also haunted by Maud of Ditchling and her lover, William de Lindfield. When Maud's husband, Lord Herbert de Hurst, discovered their love he bricked up William in a cell and left him to die, making his wife listen to her lover's moans. A skeleton was later found behind the wall!

The Grey Lady of Patcham

A Christmas ghost story, mentioned by Cecile Woodford in her *Portrait of Sussex* concerns the experiences of her father as a young man in All Saints Church, Patcham. Attending a Christmas Eve service, he saw a pale lady dressed in grey in a nearby pew who looked very cold. He spread his overcoat around her shoulders and she vanished during the singing of the final hymn, leaving his coat on the pew. He was sitting next to the door and did not see her leave. He was told locally that he had seen the Grey Lady of Patcham. Tony Wales in his *Sussex Ghosts and Legends* mentions a haunting highlighted in *The Sussex Weekly Advertiser* in 1796, of 'supernatural appearances which greatly alarmed some respectable persons' on Christmas Day each year outdoors at Patcham, on a spot where the remains of a murdered woman were subsequently found. More recently there have been several sitings of the Grey Lady in Preston Manor

Herstmonceux Castle. (*J. Greig, 1815*)

The Phantom Drummer of Herstmonceux Castle

According to Arthur Beckett's *The Wonderful Weald*, Herstmonceux Castle 'was said to have been haunted by a ghost nine feet high, which bestrode the battlements to the tuck of a drum' and walked through walls. The older version of the tale is that a Lord Dacre, who was supposed to be dead, lived concealed in the Drummers' hall and beat a mysterious drum to frighten away his widow's suitors. This tale influenced Addison's eighteenth-century play *The Drummer*, whilst the legend was itself modified by the success of the play. Horace Walpole, the Gothic novelist, visited Herstmonceux Castle in 1752, reporting that 'They showed us a dismal chamber, which they call Drummer's Hall, and suppose Mr. Addison's comedy is descended from it'.

William Axon in *Bygone Sussex* (1897) writes:

> The local story appears to have been that the martial spirit guarded a treasure placed in a chest and concealed in a recess of the wall. This hoard having been discovered by a steward of the estate the drummer felt relieved of his duty.

Beckett also mentions a later tradition that the drummer was a Frenchman pretending to be a ghost to frighten people whilst his comrades were hiding contraband goods in the castle ruins. But the legend may well precede import smuggling of contraband by organised gangs.

The Skulls of Warbleton Priory & Lade

Two skulls kept at Warbleton Priory, now part of a farm, were believed to cause sinister noises and bad luck if moved; they were said to be the skulls of the former owner of the Priory and his murderer. The Lade Screaming Skull was kept in a cupboard in the Lade family house. There were several burials of it in the churchyard, but it continued screaming until brought back to the house.

Sir Goddard Oxenbridge of Brede Place

Extraordinary legends have accumulated around the historical figure of Sir Goddard Oxenbridge of Brede Place, who died in 1537 and whose monument is in Brede Church. In legends he has been transformed into an ogre who dined upon young children. The only means of getting rid of him was to cut him in two with a wooden saw. His neighbours made such a saw, got him drunk, and cut him in half at Groaning Bridge in Stubb's Lane. Some versions of this legend say it was the children of East and West Sussex who took one end of the saw each. Mark Anthony Lower calls this story 'a wise saw'!

> *The Cavalier Lunsford of East Hoathley*
> *A legendary and ghostly cannibal:*
> *From Fielding and from Vavasour,*
> *Both ill-affected men;*
> *From Lunsford eke deliver us,*
> *That eateth up children.*

Sir Goddard's ghost haunts both the Groaning Bridge and Brede Place in the form of a body trunk. Lunsford is also mentioned by Samuel Butler in *Hudibras* and by Cleveland:

> *They fear*
> *Even his dog, that four-legged cavalier,*
> *Him that devours the scraps which Lunsford makes,*
> *Whose picture feeds upon a child in steaks.*

Squire Paulett of St Leonard's Forest

If you entered St Leonard's Forest on horseback at night you were in danger of a headless phantom jumping onto the back of your horse and joining you; this was the ghost of Squire Paulett. Arthur Beckett gives further details:

By reason of our afternoon travel we escaped the apparition of a certain Squire Paulett, and this was no small matter. In this enchanted wood it was the custom of that fearful thing to leap upon the crupper of horsemen journeying through the forest by night; and the chief cause of terror was due to the fact that, although the ghost was of human form it was, nevertheless, headless, and neither prayers nor menaces could help to shake it off the saddle until the extreme edge of the wood was reached, when forthwith it became powerless.

Nan Tuck of Rotherfield

Nan was suspected of murdering her husband. She fled towards Buxted to avoid being lynched and ran into some undergrowth and was never seen again, except as a ghost haunting Nan Tuck's Lane. After the First World War when the wood was restored, there was one patch on which no sapling would grow, despite several attempts; the locals claimed this was where Nan had disappeared.

The Campbell Family of Aldwick

There was a tradition that when a male member of the Campbell family was about to die, three ravens appear on the walls of the Castle, or wherever the doomed man happens to be. Just before Sir Duncan Campbell's death from illness, a neighbour saw 'three miserable looking, drenched ravens' on the castle roof.

The Spread Eagle Hotel, Midhurst

This medieval building has at least three ghosts. A coachman in black is seen in a bedroom built above the old coach house; The Golden Lady appears in the Edward the Seventh Room; and a Lady in Green in Tudor clothes appears in the room below.

Lady Edona, Manfred and the Ghostly Ship

According to tradition, Lady Edona lived in Brighton in the fourteenth century; her lover Manfred vowed to place the belt of St Nicholas on the tomb of the blessed Virgin in Jerusalem before marrying her, but he was drowned on the return journey, when his ship struck a rock off Worthing Point. Lady Edona witnessed the sinking, died of shock and was buried in St Nicholas churchyard. The ghostly ship is seen at midnight on May 17th each year, the anniversary of the sinking.

The Grey Lady of Michelham

In *The Wonderful Weald*, Arthur Beckett writes:

And now I must speak of the Grey Lady of Michelham. In a certain chamber of the Priory, in the dead of night, there enters, without opening the door, a lady dressed in grey silk. Slowly, and with stately steps, she walks up to the bed, withdraws the curtains and looks upon the sleeper. For a minute she gazes upon him, then, shrinking back as if disappointed, her silks rustling as she moves, she vanishes at length through the closed door.

Middle House, Mayfield

Queen Elizabeth I once slept in Middle House, which is haunted by a lady. One of the former owners is said to have locked his wife in a little room at the top of the stairs whilst he drank and carried on an affair with another woman in the rooms below. One day he forgot to lock the door, and she hit him with an iron bar and he was never seen again. His wife ran away, but her ghost haunts the house.

The White Dog

A white dog haunts the White Way road between Alfriston and Seaford every seven years on Midsummer's Eve, and it is very unlucky to see it. The dog is said to have been owned by 'Young' Chowne, heir to the Burnt House, who was killed with his dog on the trackway.

The Broadwater Skeletons

According to Charlotte Latham:

> There stood, and may still stand, upon the downs close to Broadwater, an old oak tree, that I used, in days gone by, to gaze at with an uncomfortable and suspicious look from having heard that always on Midsummer Eve, just at midnight, a number of skeletons started up from its roots, and joining hands danced round it till cock-crow, and then as suddenly sank down again.

Southover Grange in Lewes is haunted by a miser.

Pharisees and Puck

The Sussex countryfolk had a firm belief in fairies, whom they called 'pharisees', derived from the Sussex dialect habit of doubling plurals ('fairies...ies'). The most well-known Sussex story about the 'pharisees' is *The Sweating Fairies*. There are several versions, but in essence, the 'pharisees' aid a farmer or workman and he overhears them complaining that they are sweating and laughs at them. They are offended and either withhold future help or punish him. 'Puck' and 'Dobbs' were common names of Sussex fairies and they could be very helpful, especially in dairy work, but easily took offence, especially if mocked or teased. There are several place names related to Puck in Sussex, such as Pook's Hill at Alciston, Puck's Style at Hartfield, Pook Lane at Lavant, Puckscroft at Rusper, Pookryde and

Pookebourne Bridge at Cuckfield, Pookbourne, Puck's Church parlour and Pox Style Wood and Pook's Pit at Wadhurst. There is a Sussex proverb 'Master Dobbs has been helping you', used when someone has done more work than expected and referring to this house fairy. Hilaire Belloc, in *The Four Men A Farrago* (1912) recounts the story that at Hallowe'en the fairies come out into the woods to dance in 'fairy rings'.

Puck features in Rudyard Kipling's stories as a conflation of Shakespeare's hobgoblin with Sussex lore. Kipling was told by an old woman who lived at Lee Farm, of the fairies being driven out of Sussex, their last refuge being Harrow Hill, near Worthing. They finally left when the archaeologists came to dig on the hill. Harrow Hill is a small hill fort and site of some Neolithic flint mines. Three hundred years earlier Michael Drayton, in his poem *Poly Olbion*, had described the wood nymphs, 'the daughters of the Weald' being driven from St Leonard's Forest because of the iron works:

> *When as the anvil's weight,*
> *And hammer's dreadful sound,*
> *Even rent the hollow woods*
> *And shook the quency ground*

Becket: The Murderers' Table

Four Norman knights, Richard le Breton, William de Tracy, Hugh de Moreville and Reginald Fitzurse crossed the Channel on 28 December 1170 in wintry seas and rode to the archbishop's palace at Canterbury. The Normans cut Becket down with their swords, piercing his body and slicing his head, after which they returned to Sussex to one of the knights' manor house at Old Malling. According to J. M. Connell's *The Religious History of Lewes* (1931):

> The pilgrims would make their devotions at the Church of St Thomas in the Cliffe. On their way out of the town they would halt at Old Malling, and listen with bated breath while their guide told them how, on the second night after the murder of Becket, his assassins were resting in his Manor House there, and how their weapons and saddles, which had been laid on a table in the room where they sat, were thrown on the floor, and on being replaced, were thrown again, as if by an unseen hand and in abhorrence of their wicked deed.

A stone table of the period, said to be that of the legend, is on show in the Sussex Archaeological Society Collections in Lewes.

Cartagena Farmhouse

At Birdham is an attractive farmhouse called 'Cartagena', parts of which date back to the sixteenth century. Legend reports that it was built by one of Drake's sea captains with profits from the Armada wrecks. However there were very few Armada wrecks in the Channel, but

Becket's Table, 2012 Sussex Archaeological Society. (*Geoff Doel*)

Cartagena Farmhouse, Birdham. (*Geoff Doel*)

Cartagena in Spain was raided by Drake in 1586 with 'much booty' taken according to a participant. Drake shared his prize monies so there could be some truth in the story, which has got confused with the Armada campaign of two years later.

Royal Legends: Canute and Harold at Bosham

Bosham is the likely site of the famous legend of King Canute demonstrating to his sycophantic courtiers that the waves would not obey him. The earthen banks erected in Canute's time to prevent the sea from flooding fields were until recently called 'chairs' and it has been suggested that Canute had inspected these to see if they were functioning; the main street of Bosham Hoe is tidal. Canute had a favourite Manor House at Bosham, later used by King Harold and shown on the Bayeux Tapestry. Thackeray wrote a poem about this, based on the tradition of the nineteenth century:

> *From the sacred shore I stand on I command thee to retreat;*
> *Venture not, though stormy rebel, to approach thy master's seat;*
> *Ocean, be thou still! I bid thee come not nearer than my feet!*

The seventeenth century manor house behind the church is thought to use the same site. Canute's young daughter died and was buried at Bosham and in 1865 a stone coffin was found a few feet under the floor of the nave of the church, with the remains of a child of about eight years of age. A mutilated body, possibly of Harold or his father Earl Godwin, was unearthed in the nave of Bosham church in the nineteenth century. There are a number of early traditions of King Harold surviving the Battle of Hastings and becoming a monk at Waltham Abbey, Chester, Canterbury or Dover. The Canterbury version stems from a twelfth century Icelandic saga 'Heming Asliksson'. The tradition reported by Norman chroniclers that William had Harold buried by the sea shore as a talisman guardian, which could well refer to Bosham.

The Escape of Prince (later King) Charles

There are many variable legends about the historical escape of Charles II from the Sussex coast after the Battle of Worcester. It is known that the very tall king disguised himself as a woman servant during his journey to the Sussex coast, but his actual route is uncertain and key points such as bridges and fords were guarded by roundheads. Tradition has it that he drank ale at The George & Dragon, Houghton (a favourite pub of the poet Hilaire Belloc), before crossing the Arun by the ferry to Bury (as the roundhead troops left to get their rations) and possibly staying at Amberley Castle (though that might have been too obviously a Royalist site). He was nearly caught crossing the Adur at Beeding. A miller who gave food and shelter to Charles on Dyke Hill was said later to have had his windmill burnt down by Parliamentary troops. Legends describe Charles hiding at Ovingdean Grange near Rottingdean, before approaching Brighthelmstone to arrange for a boat. An old tree on the edge of the Royal Pavilion grounds in Brighton was known as 'Charles Tree' and was supposed to be where Charles and Lord Wilmot hid. A local Brighton story tells of Charles being knocked over by a fishwife in the Lanes. Thomas Horsfield gives the factual account from Brighton onwards, the escape being engineered by Colonel Gunter who hid Charles in his house at Racton, near Chichester:

> After many wanderings and hair-breadth escapes, he succeeded, through the intervention of Lord Wilmot, Colonel Gunter, of Racton, and a French merchant named Mancel, in procuring at Brighton a small vessel. He arrived at Brighton on the 13th of October, and took up his abode at the George, where he remained all night; and having embarked on board Tattersall's vessel early in the morning of the 14th of October, sailed at eight o'clock. The wind held good till the following morning, when the royal runaway arrived and landed safely at Feschamp, in Normandy.

It is fact that Charles sailed in Nicholas Tettersell's coal brig *The Surprise* (later renamed *The Escape*), from Shoreham harbour. According to another legend he sheltered in what is now called 'King Charles's Cottage' at Shoreham until boarding the boat at the last minute. Charles paid Tettersell £60 to sail him to Fécamp and after the Restoration Tettersell received further rewards and bought the Old Ship Hotel in Brighton. This is probably the origin of the legend that the disguised King stayed his last night before flight at the inn; in fact he stayed at the George Hotel, which no longer survives. Tettersell is buried in St Nicholas churchyard, Brighton.

George V

George V, when recommended Bognor as a place to convalesce is said to have responded with the immortal words 'bugger Bognor'.

Legends of a German Landing in Sussex

Legends of a German landing on the Brighton coast during the Second World War are curiously like traditions of Napoleon landing on the Dorset coast; they have an archetypal element. I come from Brighton and first heard this legend from my father who was in the Home Guard; later I collected a similar version from a retired senior police officer in the area whilst conducting a census. Both versions mentioned bodies of German soldiers being washed up on the shore. One explanation that I have been given is that this was some kind of psychological warfare with corpses floated ashore.

3

Silly ('Selig') Sussex: Religion and Folklore

Although Sussex was one of the last counties to be converted to Christianity, it soon gained a reputation for holiness and the epithet 'selig Sussex', 'selig' being an Anglo-Saxon word for 'holy'. The epithet stuck, but the true meaning of the word was forgotten and mistranslated as 'silly', with all sorts of anecdotes to explain the association. Many saints' lives are interlinked with folklore, superstitions and customs.

Saints

Dicul

Although not technically a saint, the Irish missionary Dicul at Bosham is the earliest monk linked to Sussex. Bede writes of him in his Ecclesiastical History:

> But the whole of the kingdom of the South Saxons was ignorant of the name and faith of God. There was, however, a certain monk there, of the Irish nation, by the name of Dicul, who had a very small monastery in a place which is called Boshanhamm, a spot surrounded by woods and sea. In it were 5 or 6 brethren who served the Lord in a life of humility and poverty. None, however, of the natives of the country cared either to imitate their life or to listen to their preaching.

St Crispin

St Crispin was patron saint of the Shoemakers' Guild and his day was 25 October. Henry Burstow describes the celebrations at Horsham:

> St Crispin's Day, the 25th October, used also to be well celebrated at Horsham, but it was regarded as an affair of the shoemakers, whose patron St Crispin was, and every one of them on that day could be depended upon to get thoroughly drunk in his honour. The townspeople generally were interested in the day because it was made the occasion for holding up to ridicule or execration anyone who had misconducted himself or herself, or had become particularly notorious during the year. An effigy of each offending person—frequently there were two together—was on Crispin's Day hung on the signpost of one or other of the public houses, usually in the district

where he or she resided, until the Fifth of November, when it was taken down and burnt. For several weeks before the day, people would be asking, 'Who is to be the Crispin?'

The first 'Crispin' I ever saw was hanging outside the Black Jug in North Street when I was quite a little shaver; I never heard whom it represented or what the man had done to get himself disliked. Another year the effigies of a man and his wife named Fawn, who lived in the Bishopric, were hanged up on the signpost of the Green Dragon. Together they had cruelly ill-used a boy, son of the man and stepson of the woman; they had also whipped him with sting-nettles. There they hung, each with a bunch of sting-nettles in the hand till November 5, when a hostile crowd collected, some of whom went down to Fawn's house, assaulted him, and smashed his hand-cart. For this they were summoned and fined £2 each, an amount quickly covered by public subscription.

Another year old Skiver Tulley, the bootmaker, offended his brother stitchers. I never knew what he had done, but they suspended his effigy to old Whiting's signpost, up at the beggars' lodging-house, on St Crispin's Day. Skiver came to Horsham from London, and being a particularly active and knowing member of the bootmakers' party, he was paid special honour: every evening from Crispin's Day till the Fifth of November, the gentlemen of the wax (cobblers) went up to the beerhouse, took the effigy in, and sat it down in the taproom, and then in its company all got drunk together.

Master shoemakers in Cuckfield used to give a dinner to their apprentices and employees on St Crispin's Day; in 1852 a contributor to *Notes & Queries* wrote:

In the parishes of Cuckfield and Hurstpierpoint in Sussex, it is still the custom to observe St Crispin's Day, which is kept with much rejoicing. The boys go round asking for money in the name of St Crispin, bonfires are lighted, and the day passes off in very much the same way as the Fifth of November.

At Slaugham in the 1890s there were tar barrels and fireworks on the evening of St Crispin's Day. A rhyme collected in Brighton in 1822 went:

> *If ever I St Crispin's Day forget,*
> *O, may my feet be never free from wet,*
> *But every dirty street and lane pass through*
> *Without one bit of sole to either shoe!*

St Clement

Sussex blacksmiths adopted St Clement as their patron saint and celebrated in various ways on his saints' day of 23 November, including explosions by placing gunpowder on their anvils. Further similarities with the later Protestant 5 November celebrations, which they may have influenced, were the effigies of 'Old Clem', rather like those of Guy Fawkes. Arthur Becket recorded memories of a Bramber tradition:

We used to have some proper fun with Old Clem, I can tell 'ee. The boys made a figure which was meant for Old Clem, with a wig an' beard an' pipe in his mouth, just as if 'twere a real man. Then they put un in a chair, an' after firing off their anvils, they carried un round to all the houses, an' asked for apples and beer. After they done that, they took the figure of Old Clem to to the public (bar) an' put un up agin the door while they had supper.

A favourite song at these festivities was 'Twankdillo', revived in the schools 'Singing Together booklets of the 1950s, which is where I learnt it, as did Kent traditional singer Ken Thompson, from whom my wife Fran collected it:

> *He're's a health to the Jolly Blacksmith, the best of all fellows,*
> *Who plies at his anvil while the boy blows the bellows.*
> *Which makes my bright hammer to rise and to fall,*
> *Here's to Old Cole and to young Cole and to Old Cole of All.*
>
> *Chor: Twanky dillo, twanky dillo, twanky dillo, dillo, dillo, dillo*
> *And a roaring pair of blowpipes made from the green willow.*

There is also a royalist sub-text to this song in Sussex, 'Old Cole' and 'Young Cole' referring to Charles I and Charles II (and possibly to the Old Pretender and Young Pretender). The monarchist support is shown in the final verse: 'Here's a health to King Charlie and likewise his Queen/ And to all the royal family where ever they're seen'. The Copper family also have a version of the song.

William Blake wrote a splendid epitaph for the Felpham blacksmith:

> *My sledge and hammer lie reclined;*
> *My bellows too have lost their wind;*
> *My fire's extinct; my forge decay'd,*
> *And in the dust my vice is laid;*
> *My coal is spent, my iron gone;*
> *The nails are driven—my work is done.*

St Cuthman

Charters of William the Conqueror held in France refer to Steyning as St Cuthman's Port and the church as 'St Cuthman's Church'. A Guild of St Cuthman at Chidham is referred to in 1522. The legend of St Cuthman comes from a late source Vol. iv of *Acta Sanctorum*, published at Antwerp in 1658:

St Cuthman was the son of Christian parents who lived somewhere in the south of England. In his youth he tended his father's sheep, and first exercised his miraculous powers by drawing a circle on the ground around the sheep, beyond which they would not stray. When his father died and poverty presently overtook him, he sought a new home—taking with him his invalid mother, for whom 'he constructed a machine, half couch, half wheelbarrow, which paid the double debt of a bed at home and a carriage abroad.' Travelling eastward he presently arrived at Steyning, where, as an act of thanksgiving, he built its first Christian church in 'a place lying at the base of a lofty hill, then woody, overgrown with brambles and bushes, but now rendered by agriculture fertile and fruitful, enclosed between two streams springing from the hill above.

Later versions of this story say that Cuthman was awaiting a sign from God as to where to build the church and this was received in the form of his wheelbarrow breaking. Some haymakers mocked him and Cuthman invoked a rainstorm and ever since Penfold (or Cuthman's) Field has attracted rain at haymaking. Cuthman does appear to have been vindictive! Another story tells how his oxen strayed on the land of a woman called Fippa, who seized them and would not return them. So Cuthman yoked her two sons to his cart in their place. Fippa cursed Cuthman, but he responded and she was carried into the sky by a strong wind, or in some versions swallowed by the earth. Cuthman thereupon released her sons.

Janet Pennington was told stories of St Cuthman as a child by her parents and has helpfully gathered them together in a booklet, *St Cuthman of Steyning—A Journey Through Time*. One of the additional legends is that, when building his church, Cuthman was helped by a mysterious stranger in erecting a heavy beam. When asked his name the stranger replied: 'I am he in whose name you are building this church.' Another story tells that Cuthman found the locals worshipping a sacred stone, and built his church on the spot, bearing in mind Pope Gregory's advice to Christianize pagan sites. The stone is thought to have given rise to the name 'Steyning' and to survive in the porch of the church.

One legend says that Cuthman came from Chidham, and there was something of a cult there with a Guild of St Cuthman in existence in 1522.

St Wilfrid

Wilfrid was a Northumbrian saint, educated at Lindisfarne, a controversial figure who was frequently imprisoned and banished. One of his exiles led to a stay in Sussex, from 680 to 685 or 686, where he set about converting the South Saxons to Christianity, under the patronage of their king, and was given an estate of 87 hides at Selsey, the site of the original Sussex cathedral, with 250 slaves on it, whom he manumitted as a first stage to priesthood. Then allying himself with the West Saxon Caedwalla, even against his erstwhile hosts, Wilfrid involved himself with Caedwalla's successful conquest of the Isle of Wight, where he gained vast new estates.

Our two main sources for Wilfrid in Sussex are his life by Eddius, who tends to magnify his achievements, and Bede. Eddius tells us that Wilfrid had to more or less start from scratch in his conversion of the South Saxons, and that the king of Sussex, Aethelwalh, was a pagan. But Bede, whose friend succeeded Wilfrid at Hexham, tells us that Aethelwalh had already been baptized through the recommendation of King Wulfhere of Mercia, who was present at the event, which must have been some years before Wilfrid's arrival, since Wulfhere died in 674 or 675. Bede also says that the king had married a Christian princess of the Hwicce, Eaba. But both sources agree that most of the nobility were converted by Wilfrid.

St Dunstan (924-988)

An expert jeweller and smith, he continued to practice these skills during his twenty-eight years as archbishop of Canterbury. His conflicts with Satan are described in the first chapter.

St Levina

St Levina was a virgin saint inspired by St Wilfrid and buried at Alfriston. Her relics were stolen by a French Benedictine monk called Balgerus and taken to St Winoc's Abbey at, Bergues, three miles south east of Dunkirk, where it was claimed that they effected several miracles.

St Richard

As bishop of Chichester, St Richard was renowned for his care of pastoral duties, his concern for the poor and the holiness of his life. Chichester Cathedral was in desperate need of a local saint to encourage visits and donations from pilgrims and even before his death in 1253 his chaplain, Ralph Bocking, was collecting stories about miracles concerning the holy bishop and these continued after his death; Ralph, a Dominican friar and university-trained theologian, gives a selection in his *Life of St Richard*, including the raising a shoal of mullets in the Ouse during a dearth of fish, whilst standing on Cliffe Bridge at Lewes. The canons of Chichester Cathedral applied to the pope for canonization, who appointed three church scholars to investigate the documentation and St Richard's merits and holiness. Forty witnesses testified to Richard's humility, nine witnesses testified that he did not care for fine clothes, expensive horses or rich trappings and nineteen testified that he acted with kindness and compassion towards the poor. In the interim period before canonisation in 1262, Richard's grave in the north aisle of Chichester Cathedral was treated as a holy site and a chaplain appointed to tend it. In 1276, in a ceremony attended by King Edward I, St Richard was reburied in a silver-gilt shrine covered with jewels behind the high altar. A number of healing miracles occurred at his tomb and shrine, which was destroyed during the Reformation in 1538.

Whilst Richard was in dispute with the king over whether he should be a bishop, he stayed with his friend the priest Simon of Tarring, and assisted him in the cultivation of figs, allegedly grafting a bud onto a barren fig tree. Another legend says that Richard fed 3,000 people at nearby Ferring with bread only sufficient for 90. Horsfield says in 1835 that 'Fig-orchards in this parish are very fine and fruitful' and the alleged St Richard fig garden used to be pointed out at the rear of a tea-shop; the fig garden now seems to be part of sheltered accommodation and some of the present trees probably originate from cuttings from trees from the parsonage gardens in 1745.

A legend tells that the beccafico, a small fig-eating bird of the warbler family migrates each summer from Italy to Tarring and Sompting (which also has fig trees) for one week only to eat the figs.

Above left: The Ouse and Bridge, Lewes.

Above right: The Fig Garden tea shop, Tarring, 1904.

Holy Wells

There is a dearth of information about holy wells in Sussex; they seem to have been largely erased from memory by the Protestant church (unlike in Kent) and to track them down one needs to check records such as artesian well listings. The Protestant Church is uneasy about the Catholic practice of making offerings at wells and their veneration. There is also the strong possibility of links to paganism, as water was venerated and Pope Gregory instructed the early missionaries to reuse pagan sites for Christian sites to encourage Christian attendance at familiar venues. In the case of wells, they would be re-named after the Virgin or various saints such as the Virgin's mother Anne who probably took over sites from Anu. The Protestants then discouraged the use of the saints' names. A few Sussex holy wells are quite well-known, such as two at Petworth—the Virgin Mary Spring and the Blessed Virgin Spring and St Katherine's Well near Winchelsea, which was renamed Queen Elizabeth's Well after her visit of 1573. The name Friday's Well at Burpham is thought to be a corruption either of Freya's well and linked to the worship of the Anglo-Saxon goddess of that name, or of the Anglo-Saxon saint St Frideswide; it had curative powers and was used by local priests to cure lepers. The Hermit's Well, also known as Holy Well at Buxted, also had curative properties and was associated with a cave hermitage.

Church Bells

Bosham Bell

An archetypal supernatural tale in the British Isles is the ghostly tolling of lost church bells. A Sussex variant of this tale, recorded in the nineteenth century, concerns the theft of the Bosham church tenor bell by Viking raiders in the ninth century. The monks returned to their plundered

Above left: The Virgin Mary's Spring Petworth, 1904.

Above right: Queen Elizabeth's Well Winchelsea, 1906.

Bosham Harbour, 1995. (*Geoff Doel*)

church and rang the other bells in a backward peal to curse the Vikings. The stolen bell responded from the Viking boat with a single peal and then fell through the bottom of the boat into what became known as Bell Hole, now known as Bosham Deep. Whenever the Bosham church bells ring, so the story goes, the sunken tenor bell responds from the deep, completing the octave peal. It has been suggested this effect (which has been noticed) is an echo.

A local wise man told the people of Bosham that the only way to regain the bell was to harness it to a team of pure white oxen to pull it onto the shore. This almost succeeded and the bell was glimpsed being pulled into shallow water, but one of the oxen had a single black hair and the rope broke!

Slinfold Bell

Harry Burstow, the Horsham traditional singer and bell-ringer, and John Pullen, a bell-ringer from Rudgwick, told the story of the inland loss of a bell cast in Rome and destined for York Minster via Stane Street, the former Roman road, in a bog at Alfoldean. The bell is said to have rolled off a wagon at Alfoldean Bridge, into a swamp; the ground was boggy there in former times and Jacqueline Simpson, in *The Folklore of Sussex*, records the story of how supernatural aid was invoked to rescue the bell. Stephen Peacock of Slinfold, heard the story from his father of the same name (born 1829), who had been told the story by a carter named Pete Greensfield, who worked on Dedisham Manor Farm, owners of the boggy land:

> They went to a cunning 'ooman, and she told them that if they got twelve white oxen and went to the spot at midnight, they could raise the bell. But no one was to say a word, or speak. So, the story goes, one night they went with twelve white oxen, which they hooked on to the bell in the bog. Then, just as the oxen drew the old bell to the top of the bog, one of the men shouted out:
> 'We've got the Alfold Dean gurt bell,
> In spite of all the devils in hell!'
> At that moment the chain which held it broke, the bell slipped back, and they never got it after all.

Other Sussex Bells

The church at Etchingham was originally enclosed by a moat and there is a legend of a great bell at the bottom. It is not known how it got there and it cannot be seen until six yoke of white oxen are brought to the spot to haul it out. There is a similar legend at Isfield, and at Selsey the bells of the old Saxon cathedral can be heard tolling under the sea. At Ferring there is a tradition of hearing bells from the lost village of Kingston under the sea and at Bulverhythe, near Hastings, a raking sound made by the sea in the bay to the west of St Leonards in rough seas is said to come from bells buried beneath the sea. When Hastings fishermen hear the 'Bells of Bulverhythe', they know that bad weather is approaching from the west.

There is a traditional Sussex Bells Rhyme:

> *An old woman limping,*
> *Says the bells of Clymping*
>
> *Bread and cheese on a board,*
> *Says the bells of Ford*
>
> *Come in and welcome,*
> *Says the bells of Felpham*
>
> *Hurry up or you'll be late,*
> *Says the bells of Faygate*
>
> *I'll give you a slap on the pate,*
> *Says the bells of Eastergate*
>
> *There's more rogues than honest men,*
> *Says the bells of Warbleton*
>
> *Shut the gate and clap'n*
> *Says the bells of Yapton*
>
> *Business finished, work begun,*
> *Says the bells of Alfriston*

Sussex humour is exemplified by the following story about bells given in Arthur Beckett's *The Wonderful Weald*:

One day a sexton in a certain Sussex village was showing a party of visitors over the old church. Pointing to the belfry he said: 'That bell is only rung in case of flood, a fire, a visit from the Lord Bishop of the diocese, or some other calamity.'

4
Anchorites and Hermits

Written by Fran Doel

From the eleventh century to the end of the fifteenth century a significant number of Sussex men and women opted to withdraw from secular society in order to adopt an intense Christian spiritual lifestyle. While most were content to enter into one of the four orders of Friars or great orders such as the Benedictine or Augustinian communities where they were subsumed into a monastic collective culture, a much smaller number chose to become hermits or anchorites in order to emulate the older penitential discipline of the highly admired Desert Fathers and Mothers who had lived out their lives in the wastelands of Egypt, Palestine and Syria.

In antiquity these early desert ascetics were famed for their austere practices which included such things as long contemplation, rigorous fasting and mortifications of the flesh. Early references term them 'hermits' and/or 'anchorites' but in the Middle Ages the Church saw a clearer distinction between these two groups while acknowledging that both were indeed solitaries whose needs and object was to retire (metaphorically) to a 'desert' of contemplative prayer and meditation.

Episcopal records show that both hermit and anchorite were required to obtain an episcopal licence before they could take up their 'office.' Anyone wishing to become a 'solitary' had first to obtain the consent of a priest known to him or her. An interview would follow and the priest would contact the bishop only if he considered the candidate suited to a harsh and solitary lifestyle. The bishop was free to conduct his own examination of the candidate and their ordination if accepted.

All recorded hermits in Sussex were men. Perhaps the Church felt that an unguarded woman, living a solitary lifestyle, no matter how fervent, should not be exposed to the inherent dangers of this particular calling. The majority of anchorites in Sussex on the other hand (as is the case in other English counties) were women.

One often has little more than their name and because their anchorages were generally pulled down at the Reformation, or their churches have themselves disappeared, even that archaeological information is not always available. Information from other counties indicates that some candidates were very young. Those who were older may have been widows or 'spinsters' i.e. unmarried women. It would have been important that they were always deeply religious and committed. Evidence from other areas suggests interestingly that they came from all kinds of backgrounds, and at least some were literate. Those men that did become anchorites rather than hermits were often priests who had reached the age of retirement. So perhaps they were very attached to their church and congregation. They presumably would have been literate. Priests were always supplied with a mass table in their living quarters so that they could continue to celebrate mass within their cells. It is quite possible that they continued to act as confessors and counselors in their communities from within their cells and were probably much loved and respected. There are also examples of men who had already taken religious vows in a monastery or friary.

What was obviously important was that their sense of vocation had to be rock hard; very young candidates, men as well as women, and those who had little experience of being enclosed were often asked to spend a year or even more living as a novice in a more traditional convent in order to test and strengthen their vocation. Mental stability was an important consideration—Sussex had its share of religious suicides, anorexics and self-harmers amongst the monastic communities and solitaries.

If accepted, each candidate no matter how enthusiastic and passionately infused with a need to give their life to God had to be provided with a dowry—in other words funded. The bishop could himself contribute (as did St Richard while bishop of Chichester) or draw on a network of patrons and generous benefactors which could include royalty, religious communities and rich individuals, all anxious to increase their reward in heaven by supporting an anchorite or hermit on earth. Benefactors could either donate a one-off payment, supply goods in kind such as baskets of firewood in winter, or baskets of fish in summer, or send alms or cash on a regular basis. Whatever financial support was offered had to be for the anchorite or hermit's lifetime. One Sussex anchorite appears to have brought claims against her bishop as she had not been sent food and small beer regularly over a long period. Factored into the fiscal equation was the fact that an anchorite enclosed in a cell had to be supported by a servant just as the Desert Fathers had been in the deserts.

The most evident difference between the hermit and anchorite is probably geographic. To a certain extent the hermit was permitted to retain freedom of movement in the world and could change the location of his hermitage several times (with of course his director's permission); it could be a stone built cell which was part of a chapel but it could also be a cave, a makeshift wooden hut or the corner of a ruined building in an isolated location. The anchorite on the other hand lived out his or her religious life walled up or locked into a specially built cell usually appended to the wall of a church which he or she never left alive.

In an attempt to channel and regulate the life-style of those who wished to become solitaries the Church, having accepted the candidate, provided them with a confessor and/or spiritual director to monitor and direct their physical and spiritual well-being.

Ceremonial induction rites for a hermit were devised (noticeably much simpler than those used for the anchorite or those in monastic institutions) which might be an indication that the eremetical life-style appealed to many Sussex men who had little or no education but were passionate in their desire to share the sufferings of Christ. Chaucer, in his persona of pilgrim in *The Canterbury Tales* noted that the most fervent pilgrims amongst the group of pilgrims making their way to Canterbury was the poor priest — on foot—an indication of the serious penitential intent behind his pilgrimage and a mark of his humility and piety.

During the ceremony the hermit made his vows of chastity, obedience and poverty after which part of the Service of the Dead was recited. For the anchorite the ceremony was more complicated and he or she was sprinkled with crushed chalk or earth after the same ritual prayers. This was part of the process of purification and cleansing—their necessary preparation for leaving 'the world'. They were also required to have confessed and been absolved of their sins and in a state of grace.

There is no 'one Rule' for either hermits or anchorites. Sometimes the priest or bishop tailor-made a Rule for the incumbents or used a Rule book that had been prepared for other sets of anchorites. St Richard is known to have written Rules for the anchorites in his charge. Various rules for hermits also survive, more often in English rather than Latin.

What both hermit and anchorite were required to do was maintain a celibate lifestyle and a cycle of regular prayer—a simplified form of the Divine Office as celebrated by those in monastic orders. Otherwise they did not change their name or adopt a distinctive costume that would mark them out in society.

Hermits, unlike anchorites, were often requested to undertake hard physical work such as the upkeep of roads, keeping wayside chapels in good repair, maintaining bridges or collecting and carrying combustibles up a tower for the lighting and maintaining of primitive beacons that were the warning systems for shipping.

Most anchorites were content to follow a quiet existence of contemplation, prayer and fasting. Too much contact with the community was frowned upon, but anyone could ask them for spiritual advice and they may have provided a valuable service in the community.

But life is never tidy and there are sad examples though not from Sussex, of anchorites who managed to escape their cells (though they were always caught and returned) and of hermits who simply disappeared and even of love affairs conducted through tiny letter-box type windows.

The Sussex Hermits

As one might expect there are indications that rock caves, and rock shelters were used by hermits in Sussex. Buxted has a number of such cave sites in grey sandstone and it was said a hermit was living in one of these in 1536. The date is significant—for between 1536 and 1541 England saw the suppression of the monasteries when monastic establishments were shut down and all hermits and anchorites were ordered to return to the secular world.

Camber in Sussex also had a hermitage—it was recorded that iconoclasts destroyed a statue of St Anthony here. This particular saint is significant and of interest for Anthony of Egypt was the very first of the Desert Fathers to seek out the wilderness (*c.* AD 270) and his biographer Athanasius of Alexandria had recorded and made famous the stories of his many temptations.

The names of two early hermits from the same hermitage in 'Seford' [Seaford] are known. The first, Peter, (surname unknown) appears in 1272—the year Edward I came to power. He may have been one of the king's pet charities for Hermit Peter enjoyed five years' 'protection' from the king. The second hermit, William Potel, who took over the same hermitage, tragically committed suicide in 1287, hanging himself in his cell.

In 1527 there is a record of a hermit, Simon Cote, who had a house and chapel at Westbourne in 1527; unsurprisingly the chapel was dedicated to St Anthony. Like many hermits Simon performed a valuable service to the community and may have been funded to do so; in his case he was responsible for the maintenance of a 'brygge and byways.'

There is a reference to a hermit recluse of St Cyriac, Chichester, in 1247. Today the site of the chapel is now a car park but in 1405 indulgences were promised to all who assisted the hermit; his name was Richard Petevyne. St Cyriac is one of those entertaining and no doubt apocryphal saints who has since been removed from the canon but in the thirteenth century his cult was well known. He was said to be the son of an early Christian martyr who had been put to death on the order of a 'governor of Silicia.' As a three year old child he was brought before the same official who had condemned his mother to death, and, recognizing him, promptly punched him on the ear. Enraged, the governor dashed the child onto the marble floor. Cyriac died instantly and, as a mini-martyr, went straight to heaven. Henry III was obviously a devotee of this child-saint as he personally paid for the chapel's upkeep.

Yet another hermit, this time in Arundel in 1459 made his home in a deserted lazarhouse—the Hospital of St James ad Leprosos for female lepers. It had been built in 1182 and when leprosy died out the building had been abandoned.

The Sussex Anchorites

As regards anchorites, little remains in material terms of their houses which were called 'anchorholds' as most cells were built as a two room lean-to structure adjoining the wall of a church. The cell usually stood in a graveyard and when the anchorite died, the corpse was often interred under the living room floor after a great deal of ceremony.

Much has been written of the anchorite's three windows—particularly the 'squint' through which the solitary could see the enactment of transubstantiation on the altar, This was the anchorite's all important window for while kneeling on a *prie-dieu* here she could hear mass and follow church ceremonies. The second window measured 2 feet 6 inches by 2 feet. Here the anchorite's servant could pass in food and drink, take out slops, pass in firewood and take out ashes. This window was always shuttered and heavily curtained. If the anchorite's squint was on the first floor this lower window could be used for her confession and where she would receive holy communion. A third window high up only permitted a view of the heavens.

We are fortunate that a certain amount of historic information regarding Sussex hermits and anchorites survives and in a variety of forms. There are for example from amongst the literati letters (some royal—we have already mentioned Edward I, Henry III and Richard I) indicating that monarchs as well as those from the rich mercantile classes often numbered anchorites amongst their favourite charities.

In Sussex, Richard de Wych (1197-1253), later elevated to the rank of sainthood and known simply as St Richard, while he was bishop of Chichester is known to have taken a great deal of interest in the many anchorites and hermits in his diocese for whom he was spiritually responsible. Amongst his Constitutions are his guide lines for the anchoritic life; he is dealing with anchorites in Pagham, Hardham, Houghton, Stopham and Westout and he writes to them as their spiritual director. He advises the solitaries never to entertain any person in their anchorage (with the exception of course of their confessors or visiting bishops if they insist). His concern is that their behaviour should never in any way be misconstrued. Unusually he does not allow his female anchoresses to have the custody or even the responsibility of repairing church vestments. He justifies this by suggesting that for some it might lead to a source of distraction and 'idle intercourse.'

Wills are yet another source of information. St Richard in his last testament left small legacies to five recluses and may also have lived in an anchorite cell for a short time. The poorer sections of society often left small bequests to their local solitaries in their wills.

In the church St Leonards Aldrington near Hove in the early 1400s the rector of the church (who had been in his youth a chaplain and chantry priest attached to Chichester cathedral) decided to spend his last days as an anchorite attached to his church. The request to his bishop was made twice. Eventually it was recorded that:

> on the 20th day of the month of December, in the Cathedral Church of Chichester, the Lord (Bishop) secludes Master William Bolle, his chaplain, rector of the parochial church of Aldrington in his Diocese into a certain dwelling place in the cemetery to the north of the said church; to exercise and live therein the life of an anchorite to the end of his life.

Bolle's cell (attached to the Lady Chapel) was roomy: 24 feet wide and 29 feet long; he had no patron—it was recorded that 'he lived at his own charges and expense in the abode built there by himself.' He was succeeded by Richard Lumbard, described as *'clericus'* which might indicate a university educated man and whose patron was the Archdeacon of Lewes.

Ruins of Aldrington Church. (*Print by Sparrow*)

St Botolph's, Hardham (also known as Heringham) contained one of St Richard's anchorite protégés. It is suggested that the two roomed cell (of which nothing remains) and which was abutted to the south wall of the chancel may well have been constructed of light walls of wattle and daub, and measured approximately 8 feet by 10 feet. The roof was of reed thatch.

On the south wall of the church of St John's Sub-Castro in Lewes is an inscription incised on the remains of a chancel arch which commemorates a rather more illustrious twelfth century anchorite—Magnus—of the royal house of Denmark The present church is early Victorian built in 1838 and its orientation is north-south unlike the earlier eleventh century church where Magnus was enclosed and which had the more usual east-west alignment. The inscription reads:

CLAUDITUR, HIC MILES DANORUM REGIA PAROLES, MAGNUS NOMEN EI MAGNAEA NOTA PROGENIEI, DEPONENS MAGNUM SE MORIBUS INDUIT AGNEM PERPETE PRO VITA FIT PARVULIS ANCHORITA
(Here is entombed a warrior of royal line, Magnus his name, from mighty Danish stock, resigned his title, became as the lamb, and finished life's race as a lowly anchorite).

In the thirteenth century an anchorite was enclosed in a tiny cell of the chancel wall of St Anne's church. This church was outside the town walls and its original dedication was that of St Peter and St Mary. St Richard de Wyche, bishop of Chichester left the anchorite 5 shillings. The anchoress was buried in her cell but her bones were later moved.

The anchoress Miliana in 1272 is said to have issued a complaint against the prior of Hardham, an Augustinian priory, claiming that she had not received the food and small beer that had been promised her. Though this may seem amusing to us small beer does not indicate drunkenness; it was the equivalent of fresh water. An enclosed anchorite who was not brought food and drink by her servant could not leave her anchorage and could only resort to begging. Begging for an anchorite was unseemly but starving to death in a cell was also not an interesting proposition.

Information from Steyning Museum gives details of her legal action against the prior. It was established by the court that the original prior had been so impressed by Miliana's piety that he arranged for the priory kitchen to supply her with 'two white loaves and one black loaf, one gallon and a half of ale, and one mess (dish) of cooked food daily'—exactly what his own monks received per day. However, when a new prior was elected, he chose not to send the anchoress her food and drink allowance and in addition claimed the rents from land which Miliana regarded was hers by right.

Miliana brought legal actions against the prior on three occasions, in 1263, 1272 and 1288. In 1272 she additionally had calculated all the back food and drink owed to her over the last eighteen years—with a grand total of 5,600 loaves, 5,600 cooked messes and 6,800 gallons of ale.

Her case was reviewed for six years by a jury at Lewes. Their decision was that the present prior was not obliged to provide for her as the priory had never agreed to be responsible for her funding—the offer of food and drink had initially been made by the priory as an act of charity. Miliana was also ordered to pay a fine for making 'a mischievous claim'.

All that remains of her cell today is a thirteenth century squint.

Other Sussex anchorites include a solitary at Stedham (name unknown but mentioned by Richard I): in Arundel Priory the incumbent of a cell was a Dominican friar: and in Chichester Cathedral a recluse was once enclosed in a cell at the north side of the Lady Chapel and to whom a certain William Neal left a small amount of money in his will.

In the Calendar of Papal Registers relating to Great Britain and Ireland for the years 1402—1403 and during the reign of Pope Boniface IX we have an instance of a male anchorite being given permission to change the location of his cell. This was a rare occurrence. The anchorite, John Bourne, was a friar preacher of Arundel who had found his original cell 'very inconvenient.' He also found living in poverty 'so trying.' The language of his appeal was not emotionally charged but he was obviously desperately unhappy. He was given papal licence to relocate 'to a more suitable place.' It was a kind and wise decision.

When an anchorite died, the entrance was broken open before the congregation gathered in the church and the bishop, priest and others would enter into the anchorage whereupon candles were set up and the corpse sprinkled with holy water and the grave prepared with an east–west orientation. Now came the prayers of the Office of the Dead, each psalm ending with *Requiem aeternam* instead of the more usual *Gloria Patri*. After the funeral mass (seen as a votive offering to benefit the soul in purgatory) absolution was given and the anchorite buried with his or her feet orientating towards the east to the singing of penitential psalms. The dignitaries and crowd then dispersed. After a good sweep, the cell was no doubt ready for the next incumbent.

5

From Hallowe'en to Bonfire Night

All Saints, All Souls and Hallowe'en

Before the Reformation the principal autumnal festival was Hallowtide or Hallowmass, consisting of the Feasts of All Saints and All Souls on 1 and 2 November. As often with holy days this was preceded with unofficial rituals during the night before, Hallowe'en. There are some indications through Irish and Welsh sources and through the Church's selection of these dates that this was a time of year that many pagan religions connected with the cult of the ancestors and in some Celtic areas it was originally the New Year. Hence the folk customs were usually associated with divination or visiting the graves of family members ('souling') and bonfires. W. D. Parish states in his *Dictionary of Sussex Dialect*:

> On All Saints Day, Nov 1, men dressed in black paraded the streets asking for contributions for prayers for the dead, and money was given to them for masses to be said on the following day— All Souls Day. Later on, people went from house to house with a collection box, in theory for the same purpose, but in practice it was a social affair; bread, cheese and home-made wine being given in exchange for all the latest news and gossip. Still later the custom was kept up by children who were given hop spiced buns called soul-cakes and a drink of ginger pop in return for singing:
>
> 'Soul! Soul! For a soul cake
> Pray, good mistress for a soul cake;
> One for Peter and two for Paul,
> Three for him who made us all.'

Guy Fawkes Night—November the Fifth

The Reformation led to the abolition of the holy days (and their attendant time of work) and there is a letter from Henry VIII to Archbishop Cranmer 'against superstitious practices wherein the vigil and ringing of bells all the night long upon All hallowday at night are directed to be abolished; and the said vigil to have no watching or ringing', which gives an indication of pre-Reformation practices. An Elizabethan proclamation 'that the superfluous ringing of bels at Allhallowtide and at Al Soul's Day with the two nights next before be prohibited' shows how the activities of the communities were restricted, leaving a vacuum. James I cleverly filled this gap by ordaining a public holiday on November the Fifth, with a church service, ringing of bells and celebrations of the survival of the royal family and parliament from the machinations of the Gunpowder Plot. In January 1606 Parliament passed 'An Acte for a publique Thancksgiving to Almighty God everie yeere on the Fifte day of November' and that the plot's discovery should 'be held in perpetual Remembrance' and that November 5th be observed as 'a holiday for ever in the thankfulness to God for the deliverance and detestation of the Papists'. The Act made provision for a special prayer to be offered up each year during morning service in every parish church: The Book of Common Prayer for 1821, has 'A Form of Prayer with Thanksgiving to be used Yearly upon the Fifth Day of November':

> Be thou still our mighty Protector, and scatter our enemies that delight in blood. Infatuate and defeat their consuls, abate their pride, assuage their malice, and confound their devices. Strengthen the hands of our gracious Sovereign, and all that are put in authority under him, with judgement and justice, to cut off all such workers of iniquity, as turn Religion into Rebellion, and Faith into Faction; that they may never prevail against us, or triumph in the ruin of thy church among us.

The folk celebrations thus inevitably had an anti-Catholic element, including the burning of Guy Fawkes in effigy and, in some areas, the burning of an image of the 1605 Pope thought to be implicated in the Gunpowder Plot. The Sussex celebrations have proved the most enduring and most spectacular in the country, particularly in Lewes, with an ongoing controversy about these anti-Catholic elements. Have they been just traditional practices, or a camouflage for Protestant propaganda?

The Oldest Guy in the World—Battle Bonfire Society, 1987. (*Geoff Doel*)

The Battle Bonfire Society claims to have world's oldest guy—the head is made of pear wood and thought to be seventeenth century, though the horsehair body is late nineteenth century. There is a very early reference to a seasonal bonfire at Battle in a churchwarden's account of 1686, where seventeen shillings and sixpence were 'expended at Gunpowder treason' for 'rejoicings'. Gunpowder was made at nearby Pepperingeye between 1676 and 1874, begun by one of the churchwardens who authorized the bonfire expenditure cited above. Effigies of Guy Fawkes were often carried in procession through villages; Sir Humphrey Repton wrote to Sir Harry Fetherstonhaugh of Uppark: 'I cannot walk ten yards and am obliged to be carried like Guy Faux on the 5th Nov'.

Bonfire Night at Lewes

Anti-Catholic feeling was strong in the early celebrations, particularly in Lewes, where the burning of seventeen Protestant Martyrs by 'Bloody Mary' was undoubtedly a powerful factor in the intensity of the celebrations. This was re-fuelled by the defection of clergy during the Oxford Movement. In 1850 a Papal Bull proclaimed the restoration of the Catholic hierarchy in England, Cardinal Wiseman being created archbishop of Westminster. There was strong Protestant concern about these events and speeches made by the mock clerics at the bonfires attacking them.

A 1679 account describes a mock religious procession through the town before burning an effigy of the Pope. In 1723 An entry in a churchwarden's account book in Lewes records a payment of two shillings and six pence to 'ye ringers being ye day of Deliverance from ye powder plott'. In 1775 the Riot Act was read and 9 ringleaders of disturbances were sent to

Lewes Bonfire Society Effigies at the John Harvey Tap. (*Geoff Doel*)

the House of Correction. In 1785, the Hampshire Chronicle describes an unsuccessful attempt by magistrates to prevent the building of a bonfire on School Hill, resulting in an evening of riot 'accompanied with the firing of rockets, squibs, grenades etc.' Further reports in 1797 and 1798 making reference to a bonfire on School Hill indicates this was a customary practice. The *Sussex Weekly Advertiser* complained of the risk of fire in Lewes High Street in 1797. In 1806 eighteen Bonfire Boys were arrested and the bonfire was moved to Castle Bank.

The rolling of blazing tar barrels through the High Street is recorded for the first time in 1832. And in 1837 the *Sussex Weekly Advertiser* describes how '20 barrels were alight at once and, having been dragged by the mob through the streets' were used to form a bonfire opposite the County Hall. In 1841, police officers were set upon 'with force and arms to wit sticks, stones, bludgeons and other offensive weapons.' Superintendent Fagan was 'struck on the head with a boulder, knocked down with bludgeons, and trampled upon'.

A detailed account of the celebrations in the *Sussex Weekly Advertiser* in 1846 shows how they were getting out of control:

> … disguised persons in several parties and accompanied by a large mob occupied themselves during the early hours of the evening by dragging burning tar barrels through the main thoroughfare of the town and building a bonfire outside of the County Hall … the tar barrel party … repaired about ten o'clock to the house of Mr Blackman, who, as an active and conscientious magistrate was well known to be opposed to the lawless proceedings of the bonfire rioters. Here the Boys built a large bonfire of tar barrels, but when Mr Blackman, alarmed for the safety of his property … went out and mildly, but firmly, desired the mob to disperse he was met with derisive jeers, and fresh means were used to increase the flames. On attempting to take one of the ringleaders into custody, which, when he had nearly accomplished he received a blow over the eye and was felled to the ground. Mr Blackman was picked up and carried into the house in a state of insensibility.

In 1847, London police were called in and 170 local tradesmen and gentry were sworn in as special constables. In the early hours of Guy Fawkes' day local constables arrested 8 men who were attempting to drag a lighted tar barrel down St Anne's Hill towards the High Street:

> No sooner had the clock struck twelve on Thursday night, the Guy Fawkes Day thus commenced, than a lighted tar barrel, held by a chain passed through it, was set rolling down the steep part of St Anne's Hill towards the High Street preceded by a man armed with a pick axe and disguised by a mask, and followed by about eighty others armed with bats and bludgeons, shouting and making an awful uproar.

At noon 80 London Police arrived and at 4 p.m. the special constables assembled. By 8 p.m. a large crowd had assembled outside County Hall. The Brighton mail coach horse was frightened by a squib and Lord Chichester read the Riot Act on the steps of County Hall and the crowd was dispersed.

M. A. Lower, an influential figure, advocated that action be taken to rid 'the town of Lewes of this abominable and disgraceful nuisance' and the *Sussex Advertiser* condemned the celebrations as 'riotous and brutalising orgies celebrated by a class of men taken from amongst the lowest ranks of society.' Lower misunderstood the disguise and face-blacking which are a part of the ritual and not to assist malefactors to be unrecognised. However, Baxter, the Conservative editor of The *Sussex Agricultural Express* sided with the Bonfire Boys and wrote that: 'We by no means agree with those who, from political motives, would put down the "Guys".' So we have the Liberal press condemning Bonfire and the Tory press supporting it. Interestingly, the shopkeepers, who in other contexts would be against disorder and rowdy behaviour and loss of income through early closing, often supported Bonfire because of their anti—Catholic stance. But the nonconformist sects seemed to be opposed to the celebrations; in 1847 many of the 32 influential townspeople signing a petition to the magistrates requesting that action be taken to suppress the celebrations were members of nonconformist sects.

In 1848, the Conservative supporters of bonfire organised a compromise. A committee of local tradesmen arranged a field for the fire site and faggots for the bonfire and a band to entice spectators from the High Street to the bonfire site in Wallands Park. But in 1850, a Papal Bull proclaimed the restoration of the Catholic hierarchy in England, Cardinal Wiseman being created archbishop of Westminster. This re-created a suitable climate for the Bonfire Boys. In the Cliffe, barrels appeared in the streets and a fire was started at 7 p.m. at Cliffe Corner. In the High Street a fire was lit outside County Hall and a crowd of 3,000 gathered to hear an oration condemning papal aggression delivered by a 'representation of Cardinal Wiseman dressed in red from top to toe.' And in 1851 effigies of the Pope & Wiseman were paraded and burnt.

The situation was resolved by the founding of the Bonfire Societies from about 1853, who took responsibility for keeping their own members under control, but united in a Grand Procession of all the societies down St Mary's Lane and into Southover, Southover High Street, up St Mary's Lane and into the High Street, where a bonfire was held in front of County Hall. In 1853, between 9.30 and 10 p.m. the Grand Procession left the Pelham Arms and approached the fire. The band was followed by a large banner bearing the inscription 'NO POPERY'. It progressed down School Hill, into Albion Street, up East Street, into Market Street and back into the High Street to the fire. A man in 'full canonicals' then addressed the crowd and an effigy of the Pope suspended over the fire. The crowd then went to a firework display on Mount Pleasant. At midnight the High Constable announced the end of the celebrations and the fire was extinguished.

The tradition of burning 'public enemies' of bonfire seems to have started in the 1850s with the burning in effigy of the emperor of Russia, enemy in the Crimean War, by the Cliffe Bonfire Society on Cliffe Corner, the *Sussex Agricultural Express* in 1855 reporting that 'they adjourned to Cliffe Corner where in an enormous Bonfire they consumed an effigy of the Emperor'. An effigy of the Pope was mentioned in 1857, secondary to 'an excellent effigy of Nana Sahib with child in one hand and bloody dagger in the other'. Four effigies appeared in 1858, among them a Pope which was 'above six feet high attired in a long white gown with a sugar loaf hat', Guy Fawkes and a High Churchman (branded locally as a papist.) In 1859 the effigy bore the inscription 'the man that stole the moneybox—November 5th 1858'. In 1860 a schoolmaster—Thomas Hopley—who had beaten a lad to death was burnt in effigy along with the king of Naples.

In 1855 there is the first reference to a tar barrel being thrown into the Ouse, a tradition that still continues. After the First World War it became customary for each society to throw a blazing tar barrel into the Ouse. In 1857 the Commercial Square Society was formed, and

'The Town' changed its name first to 'Lewes' then to 'Borough'. Waterloo's first existence was 1857-8. There was a St Anne's Society from 1876-1880 and Southover was formed in 1886 and South Street Juveniles in 1913. In 1869 there was a further religious controversy affecting Bonfire—the building of a Roman Catholic chapel in Lewes, which was drawn attention to by a tableaux being paraded, and later exploded.

The Cliffe programme of 1870 stated that over 40 barrels would be burnt during the evening, including 8 large hogsheads and 6 tar barrels in the 9 o'clock procession. Later special 4 wheeled carts were made to carry the barrels, made of iron and 3 large barrels could be chained on to each one. Two still exist. One is in the museum at Anne of Cleves House and the other leads the Grand Procession.

In 1871 the tableau was 'illustrative of a Brighton poisoning case'. *The Daily Telegraph* described the 1875 celebrations:

I saw that the principal bonfire was to be lit opposite the County Hall. Having engaged rooms at the White Hart, immediately opposite, I found by pacing the roadway between the two buildings, that the width was 36 feet...The procession containing Pope Pius IX, Guy Fawkes and the homicidal Chinaman (the reputed murderer of Commodore Goodenough) started at half-past nine, there having been several previous processions of less note, the bonfires blazing all the while, and being replenished from time to time by tar barrels run on tumbrils through the town... There were people in long white bed gowns, in grotesque tunics ... other people wonderfully dressed as sages ... and yet others who simply wore masks and tinsel ... the great 'No Popery' banner, attended by the Borough Bonfire Society's brass band ... When the procession had marched round the bonfire, and the bishop had read a mock service and delivered a fiery exhortation, the three gigantic effigies were brought up, amid howls and execrations.

The report goes on to describe how, once the fireworks that were stuffed in the effigies were ignited, the burning remains were thrown onto the fire, which was kept blazing until well after midnight. Fire was a fear and the Bonfire Societies tried to ally concern by banning the notorious homemade squib, the 'Lewes Rouser', and by restricting the size of the tar barrels dragged through the streets.

The Cliffe Bonfire Society has always been somewhat independent of the other societies, with its own procession to the fire distinct from the Grand United Procession. T. F. Thiselton-Dyer in 1876 recorded the words chanted at the Bonfire Society's 'Prayers':

Remember, Remember, The Fifth of November
The Gunpowder Treason and Plot;
I see no reason why Gunpowder Treason
Should ever be forgot.
Guy Fawkes, Guy Fawkes, t'was his intent
To blow up the King and the Parliament
Three score barrels of powder below
Poor old England to overthrow;
By God's providence he was catch'd
With a dark lantern and burning match.

Holla boys, holla boys, make the bells ring,
Holla boys, holla boys, God save the King.

A penny loaf to feed the Pope,
A farthing o' cheese to choke him.
A pint of beer to rinse it down
A faggot of sticks to burn him!
Burn him in a tub of tar,
Burn him like a blazing star,
Burn his body from his head
Then we'll say old Pope is dead!
Hip, hip, hoo-r-r-ay.

Towards the end of the nineteenth century new efforts at suppression were made. In 1884, W. K. Armstrong, the minister at Eastgate Baptist Church, in a letter to *The Times*, said that the night is characterised by 'licentiousness and drunkeness' and was a carnival of sin'. Protestant extremists, some from the Orange Order and some actual clergymen addressed crowds at the bonfire sites with anti-Catholic propaganda. But others dressed up as mock Roman Catholic clerics to satirise the Papacy's political interference in Britain. Traders continued generally to support, or turn a blind eye, to riotous behaviour because they were protestant and the burnings of 'Bloody Mary' had a long and awful legacy in intolerance.

There was a positive tableau 'Honour to Mr Plimsoll' featured in 1875 and a neutral one drawing attention to the problem of 'The Great Eastern Question' in 1896. The anti-Catholic sentiments remained strong at the end of the nineteenth century. 'No Popery' banners were carried, effigies of the Pope were burnt by all societies and anti-Catholic speeches were by the mock-clerics, such as 'The Bishop of Newtown'; 'The Lord Bishop of the Cliffe' and 'His Grace the Archbishop of St John-sub-Castro'. The bishop of Cliffe said in 1874: 'what the Catholics aspire to is universal dominion all over the world, with the Pope at their head'. In 1901 the Martyrs' Memorial was dedicated to the 17 protestant martyrs who were burnt at the stake outside the Star Inn between 1555 and 1558. The Reverend Glandfield at Southover's fire in 1904 stated that:

They were opposed by a religion, or rather a political organisation, which aimed at the destruction of the liberty of England and was straining every nerve to crush Protestantism out of the land … the Romanish doctrine, imperceived, is stealing our nation like an eclipse of the sun.

During the early days the effigy of the Pope was usually the current one, but in 1902 at the Commercial Square Bonfire Society dinner, the secretary stated that the society 'did not burn the effigy of the present pope, but that of Pope Paul V, who was the head of the Romish Church at the time of the Gunpowder Plot.'

In Oct 1905 there was a petition against the Bonfire Societies, attacking them for risk of fire, immorality and drunkenness, signed by 94 inhabitants, many members of the strong temperance movement in Lewes. It was submitted to the joint standing committee of East Sussex County Council, bypassing the town council, which was more sympathetic to bonfire, with at least four town councillors being associated with bonfire societies. A counter-petition

Lloyd George burnt in effigy, Bucks Green, 1909. (*The 'People's Budget'*)

signed by 492 inhabitants from Lewes and 287 persons from surrounding villages was presented. The *Sussex Agricultural Express* reported that the 1905 celebrations went off peacefully and:

> provided a series of gorgeous spectacles, which gave the utmost pleasure to thousands … and the splendid order and good humour which was observed throughout the evening was the effective answer to those who urge that the celebrations should be suppressed.

A town councillor and alderman George Holman spoke up in favour of bonfire:

> In these days of utilitarianism … many old English sports have fallen into abeyance … which is owing principally, I think to the platitudes and sophistry of goody-goody people … in an old town like Lewes, which is saturated with old customs and traditions that conduce to make it as a contrast to the prosaic manner in which some of the towns have gone I think they should retain all these customs that are harmless and amusing to the people.

A fire in the High Street in 1904 raised concerns about the locations of the bonfires and the letting off of fireworks near timber buildings, and there was a petition to suppress the celebrations. The bonfire societies attempted to allay these fears by issuing notices condemning the use of the 'Rouser' squib and by restricting the size of the tar barrels which they dragged through the streets. Each society at that time had its fire in the principal street of their area—the Borough outside the County Hall, Cliffe at Cliffe Corner, Commercial Square in Commercial Square and Southover outside the King's Head in Southover High

Crawley Guy Fawkes Bonfire 1914—the last one to be built in the roadway.

Street. Eventually the bonfires were moved to the outskirts of the town and a Sussex byelaw made this a general provision, so that by the 1980s only the Battel Bonfire Boyes had a fire-site in the town centre, as English Heritage, which owned the Abbey site, were unaffected by the bye law. The police then moved the Battle site further out of town; I was there on this occasion and thought that the new site was far more dangerous of access on a poorly lit road and onto a darkened field through hedges than the highly visible and convenient earlier site. The police and councils sometimes seemed anti-bonfire and to cause more problems than they solved; the bonfire societies themselves have been generally responsible in responding to problems and orderly on the night.

In 1906 fires and tar barrels were banned from Lewes town centre. A torchlight procession with fancy dress was allowed. The Southover Society, unable to find an alternative site, suspended operations. The Borough amalgamated with Commercial Square who had been loaned a site along the Brighton Road. Cliffe moved their firesite to Malling Fields. A token gesture was made to build a bonfire in Commercial Square on 5 November 1906; those concerned were arrested, charged and acquitted. Instead of fires in the streets, each society carried a blazing tar barrel to Cliffe Bridge.

In 1973 the Cliffe Society realised that the scarcity of wooden barrels, which only last one procession, was a problem and they constructed barrel carts using 45 gallon drums, which last all evening. Satirical effigies continued to be hugely popular and effective. During the twentieth century these included the Kaiser, the Russian Bear, Makarios, an Arab highjaker, Michael Foot, Ronald Regan (wearing a ten-gallon hat complete with rotating cruise missiles), Ian Paisley, Argentinian soldiers paddling a giant tin of Fray Bentos corned beef, Scargill & Macgregor together, Margaret Thatcher dressed in pink chiffon and Union Jack knickers,

Lewes Bonfire celebrations 2014 effigy of Vladimir Putin. (*Social Bonfire*)

Miterrand and Rainbow Warrior in 1985, the South African president in 1986 and the Ayotollah in a bath tub playing with boats in 1987 and Tony Blair. In the twenty-first century targets have included Angela Merkell, President Putin, David Cameron, Alex Salmon and Kim, Boris Johnson, and Nigel Farage. There are also local enemies of bonfire who are paraded in effigy.

Each bonfire society consumes thousands of torches. Work begins on preparing these in the summer. A stick about 3 feet long has combustible material (used to be tow, now old carpet underfelt often used) wrapped round one end to form a head which is held in place with wire. A notch or split in the end of the stick prevents the head slipping down the stick.

Often between thirty and forty thousand spectators pour into Lewes and handling these is now the main problem, particularly due to drink and rowdy behaviour. Access to fire-sites is usually charged for and numbers controlled, but the early part of the evening, with processions in the High Street with banners, morris dancers, Zulu warrors, smugglers and jazz bands is free and very lively and vivid. The genuinely anti-Catholic elements have declined and the focus is on patriotism, 'enemies' being those who have caused (like Guy Fawkes and his co-conspirators) or are causing problems for the liberty and well-being of the British people. Many Roman Catholics now belong to bonfire societies, but others are uneasy at what they see as a ritualistic and emblematic attack on the Papacy, even if this is historic and validated to some extent by customary right/rite.

6

The Winter Solstice and Celebration of Christmas

Christmas celebrations in Sussex are rooted in a blend of Germanic paganism and enthusiastic early Christianity. They are linked to solsticial and New Year festivities and rituals, with the Church choosing a date to celebrate the birth of Christ which enabled it to absorb earlier pagan beliefs and celebrations.

Wassailing, from the Anglo-Saxon 'waes hael' (be healthy) and of pagan origin, was noted in the north of the county in the nineteenth century and the Yule log and apple wassailing survived on the Weald and at the village of Duncton respectively until the early twentieth century. The Christmas evergreens and mistletoe also originally relate to pagan midwinter, solsticial and New Year celebrations which were taken over by emerging Christianity. Feasting is another element of the ancient Yule festivities which has survived into medieval and modern Christian Christmas celebrations.

Rudyard Kipling's famous poem *Eddi's Service* excellently captures the spirit of the earliest Anglo-Saxon phase of Sussex Christianity, connected with the conversion of parts of Sussex by St Wilfrid and his biographer, St Eddius, and speculates on the early Christmas services:

'Eddi's Service'

Eddi, priest of St Wilfrid
In the chapel at Manhood End,
Ordered a midnight service
For such as cared to attend.

But the Saxons were keeping Christmas,
And the night was stormy as well.
Nobody came to service
Though Eddi rang the bell.

'Wicked weather for walking,'
Said Eddi of Manhood End.

Church Norton. (*Geoff Doel*)

But I must go on with the service
For such as care to attend.'

The altar candles were lighted,—
An old marsh donkey came,
Bold as a guest invited,
And stared at the guttering flame.

The storm beat on at the windows,
The water splashed on the floor,
And a wet yoke-weary bullock,
Pushed in through the open door.

'How do I know what is greatest,
How do I know what is least?
That is My Father's business,'
Said Eddi, Wilfrid's priest.

But, three are gathered together —
Listen to me and attend.
I bring good news, my brethren!
Said Eddi, of Manhood End.

And he told the Ox of a manger
And a stall in Bethlehem,
And he spoke to the Ass of a Rider
That rode to Jerusalem.

They steamed and dripped in the chancel,
They listened and never stirred,
While, just as though they were Bishops,
Eddi preached them The Word.

Till the gale blew off on the marshes
And the windows showed the day,
And the Ox and the Ass together
Wheeled and clattered away,

And when the Saxons mocked him,
Said Eddi of Manhood End,
'I dare not shut his chapel
On such as care to attend.'

But, as we have seen, there was an earlier Celtic missionary Dicul at Bosham who was perhaps the first to celebrate the midwinter Christmas in Sussex. There was a miraculous Christmas cure at Richard's tomb in Chichester Cathedral, the most important Sussex pilgrimage site.

The Chichester Boy Bishops

During the thirteenth century a strange tradition arose among the choirboys in a number of cathedrals and parish churches; it was practised at Chichester and endured until the Reformation, On 6 December, the feast of St Nicholas, patron saint of children, one of the boy singers was chosen to become a 'mock bishop'. He was ceremonially dressed in scaled down scarlet bishop's robes and given a mitre and miniature crozier and for a three-week period (until 'Childermass', the feast of the holy innocents, 28 December) was treated with mock respect as a 'pretend' bishop, being led in procession through the crowded streets at Christmastime and 'presiding' over services which took place in the choir. Some 'boy bishops' even delivered a Christmas sermon. This could not have been effected without the full approval and connivance of the choirmaster and bishop. It also demonstrates that the Christmas season was perceived in the medieval period as being a merry and light-hearted time and that children were included in the fun. St Nicholas, on whose feast day the boy bishops were elected, was a fourth century bishop of Myra, and is the forerunner of our Santa Claus. His gift of gold to three poor girls as dowries, is regarded as the forerunner of the Christmas present. The Chichester Cathedral accounts for 1534/35 include an: 'Item for new makyng the robe of scarlet for the chyld boysshop Lawrence 10*d*'.

Lord of Misrule at Chichester

The Lord of Misrule is another 'inversion' custom which invites a healthy, but short-lived critique of office and order by standing it on its head. During the middle ages a 'Lord of Misrule' was commonly elected in castles, monasteries and other communities to promote mirth and merriment. They presided over bizarre activities in which order was inverted—but only over the Twelve Days of Christmas for then their 'rule' and authority ended. The post and its traditions may owe something to the Roman feast of Saturnalia, where order and proprietary were also overturned and inverted.

The following brief account comes from the sixteenth century records of Chichester consistory courts. On a cold winter's night on 30 December 1586, one William Brunne, an elected Lord of Misrule, was visiting his local inn, the Swan, when he came across a Mr Weston, a visitor to Chichester. Seeing an occasion for seasonal fun, Brunne, exacted 'a fun penance' from Mr Weston, who was on official business from the Admiralty; and obliged him to submit to the indignity of riding a broomstick from the inn to the town cross at nine o'clock at night. The town cross at Chichester (built at the expense of Edward Story, Bishop of Chichester in 1500), is found at the junction of the four main streets in the city. An ornate stone octagonal building now without the cross which once surmounted it and gave the building its name, it was originally designed for the 'use and benefit of the poor', to afford them shelter and protection from sun and rain 'when they frequented the market':

> Mr H. Weston 4th day of March 1586/7 appeared and objected to the charge that he played at tables all night in an Inn in the city of Chichester publicly to the slander of his function. He alleged that he was sent for by virtue of a Commission from my Lord Admiral to be examined about certain marine causes the 30th day of December last and being in the town somewhat late so that he could not be dispatched to return home again the same night, he went to the sign of the Swan for lodging where being on the next day in the morning about eight of the clock he played at the tables with the goodman of the house and he had not played above an hour's space but that one, perforce took this examinate from thence and made him ride over a staff to the Cross.

Gooding and Doles

On St Thomas's Day (21 December) women, particularly widows, went 'a gooding' from door to door collecting money (or in some cases food and drink) which they used to celebrate, sharing out what remained after the celebrations. Horsfield in the *History and Antiquities of Lewes* (1827) mentions it as being particularly observed in the Lewes neighbourhood. W. D. Parish, in his *Dictionary of Sussex Dialect*, says 'a widow had a right to a double dole' and that 'the presumed object was to obtain money or provisions for the approaching festival of Christmas'. And the Sussex social historian M. A. Lower commented in 1861:

> Formerly the old women of every parish went from house to house to beg something to provide for the festivities of Christmas. The miller gave each dame a little flour, the grocer a few raisins, the butcher an odd bit of beef, and so on. For persons not in trade a donation in money was expected.

A 'Gooding' custom is also recorded at Beeding, where the vicar 'doled' out a silver coin to any elderly women who brought him a sprig of evergreen. And Henry Burstow of Horsham in his *Reminiscences* remembered large amounts of food being given to poor people going 'a gooding', including joints of meat, plum puddings and tea. In the Cliffe district in Lewes, in a draper's shop there was a large box full of old hats labeled 'For the Gooders'.

St Thomas's Day was also a favourite for charitable bequests in order to give the poor some food and money for Christmas. Thomas Turner helped to administer the Pelham Dole and gives an account of this in his diary for 1759:

> Friday Dec 21—We arose at three, to perform our task, viz: some of the ancestors of he Pelham family have ordered that, on this day (for ever) there should be given to every poor man or woman that shall cum to demand it, 4*d* and every child 2*d*; and also to each a draught of beer, and a very good piece of bread. I believe there was between seven and eight hundred people relieved of all ages and sexes, and near £9 distributed, besides a sack of wheat made into good bread, and near a hogshead and half of very good beer.'

Christmas Fare

From the journal of a Sussex gentleman, Timothy Burrell, Esquire, Barrister-at-law of Ockenden House, Cuckfield, which he kept between the years 1683 to 1714, we learn that in the early eighteenth century the 'cannon ball' form of the Christmas plum pudding had not yet made an appearance—then the tradition was to serve 'plum pottage' (also known as plum porridge or plum broth)—which Burrell had served up to his thirteen guests (apparently a 'mix' of the servant class and 'gentlemen') in between courses no less than three times during the same Christmas feast.

Charles Fleet in his book *Glimpses of our Sussex Ancestors* comments on Burrell's entry for 1704:

> One of the most prominent features of Mr Timothy Burrell's Journal—and it marks the benevolence of his character and illustrates the close relations which once existed between the high and lower classes of society, whom he invited to dine with him at Christmas, and the bills of fare that he provided for them. He commenced this custom in 1691, and he keeps it up to the year before his death (1717). The following are the bills of fare for the Burrell Christmas Dinner of 1706:

> 1st January, 1706.

> Plumm pottage, calves' head and bacon, goose, pig, plumm pottage, roast beef, sirloin, veale, a loin, goose, plumm pottage, boiled beef, a clod (?), two baked puddings, three dishes of minced pies, two capons, two dishes of tarts, two pullets.
>
> It will be remarked that plum pudding, without which no Christmas-day festivities would now be complete, does not figure in Mr Timothy Burrell's bill of fare. Its place is supplied by 'plumm potage' (sometimes called 'plumm broth') which occurs thrice in each bill, and which no doubt stood in the place of, and was the embryo of its more famous ancestor. Minced pies had arrived at maturity; but plum pudding had yet to be invented.

E. V. Lucas in his book *Highways and Byways in Sussex*, 1928 supplies an old recipe for Plum Porridge:

Plum Porridge, it may interest some to know, was made thus: Take of beef-soup made of legs of beef, 12 quarts; if you wish it two be particularly good, add a couple of tongues to be boiled therein. Put fine bread, sliced, soaked, and crumbled; raisins of the sun, currants and pruants two pounds of each; lemons, nutmegs, mace and cloves are to be boiled with it in a muslin bag; and a quart of red wine and let this be followed, after half an hour's boiling, by a pint of sack. Put it into a cool place and it will keep through Christmas.

William Thompson's Personal Account of the Lewes Avalanche, written about 1870, describes the poignant ruin of Christmas food and decorations which, whilst heightening the horror of the circumstance, gives us a glimpse of the seasonal festivities of ordinary people in Lewes at this period, showing that even slightly before the advent of the influence of Victoria and Albert, small houses had their own individual decorations and Christmas fare:

The furniture and clothes of the poor sufferers were mixed in utter confusion with broken roofs, black bricks from chimneys and ruined crockery while occasional pieces of cake and plum pudding, intermingled with holly and evergreens, exhibited bitter memorials of the festivities of Christmas.

The first literary mention of the Sussex 'Kissing Bough' or 'Kissing Bunch'—circles of suspended evergreen boughs formed into circles and decorated with candles and red apples, with mistletoe in the centre, appeared in the seventeenth century.

Wassailing and Apple Wassailing

Geoffrey of Monmouth, in 1136, tells the story that the term was first used in Britain by the daughter of the Saxon mercenary leader Hengist, Renwein (Rowena in later versions) to greet the British King Vortigern, who desired and married her. The tradition of wassailing was a midwinter visitation ritual to bring good fortune for the ensuing year and consisted of a procession of wassailers carrying a wassail bowl from door to door and singing songs which asked for food, drink and money and wished good luck to the household. Many elaborate wassail bowls survive from the middle ages and the custom continued well into the eighteenth century and has not completely died out. But in the late eighteenth century and nineteenth century, wassailing was gradually replaced by carol singers singing religious carols, though sometimes with the odd wassail song in their repertoire. A tradition of wassailing survived at the Elephant and Castle pub at West Chiltington at Christmastime until the First World War, and was photographed in 1910.

The wassail songs were not religious, but sometimes their tunes are associated with carols. Thus the tune of *God Rest Ye Merry Gentleman*, in the ancient Dorian mode (i.e. key of D using the white notes only on a piano), is very similar to *The Sussex Wassail* collected by a Sussex vicar, John Broadwood, when it was sung on his doorstep by some boy mummers. John Broadwood published this in his *Old English Songs from the Weald of Surrey and Sussex* in 1843:

'The Sussex Wassail'
A wassail, a wassail, a wassail we'll begin
With sugar plums and cinnamon and other spices in.

Chorus: With a wassail, a wassail, a jolly wassail
And may joy come to you and to our wassail

Good Master & good Mistress as you sit by the fire
Remember us poor wassail boys who travel through the mire

Good Master & good Mistress if you should be quite willing
Pray send us out your eldest son with six pence or a shilling

If there's any maids within this house as I suppose there's none
They'd not let us stand a wassailing so long on this cold stone

We'll cut a slice all from the loaf and set it by the fire
We'll wassail bees and apple trees until your heart's desire

We've wassailed all this day long and nothing could we find
But an owl in an ivy tree and her we left behind

Our shoes are very dirty, or shoes are very thin
They lack a little silver to line them well within

Hang out you silver tankard upon you're golden spear
We'll come no more a-wassailing until another year

The words of the song firmly locate it as a wassail rather than a religious carol. Christ and Mary are not mentioned, but the song is concerned with food and drink and the annual cycle of sympathetic magic effecting good luck. As well as the door to door wassailing tradition, the song also invokes wassailing bees and apple trees, both of which traditionally occurred in Sussex. The vicar of Amberley, the Rev. G. Clarkson, collected the words of a song thought to have been sung to the bees on Twelfth Night from an old man in his parish:

Bees, oh bees of paradise, does the work of Jesus Christ.
Does the work which no man can,
God made bees and bees made honey.
God made man and man made money.
God made great men to plough and to sow.
God made little boys to tend the rooks and crows.
God made women to brew and to bake.
And God made little girls to eat up all the cake.
Then blow the horn!'

Essentially, though, the words of *The Sussex Wassail* convey the cold and damp condition of the wassailers as they trudge from house to house and wait on the doorsteps in the hope of the food and drink and money which seal the good luck compact between householders and seasonal wassailers.

Apple Wassailing—the 'Duncton Howlers'

Apple wassailing, or howling as it was termed in Sussex because of the din, is a piece of sympathetic magic which used to be prevalent in cider apple districts of England in which a libation of cider punch was given each year to a representative cider apple tree to invoke a bountiful crop of cider apples. In the west of England male orchard workers tended to wassail their own trees, often firing guns, either to arouse the tree or frighten away evil spirits. But in Sussex semi-professional groups of boys, known as 'howling boys' moved from orchard to orchard in specific locations between Christmas Eve and Twelfth Night to wassail trees for money, food and drink. Sussex has the first recorded specific reference in the country (not counting a general allusion in a poem by Robert Herrick) when Giles Moore, rector of Horsted Keynes recorded in his diary for 26 December 1670: 'Gave to the howling boys 6d'. And Timothy Burrell of Cuckfield wrote in his diary in 1691: 'A shilling paid to Howlers on New Year's Eve'.

Charlotte Latham mentions the custom in her book *Some West Sussex Traditions Lingering in 1868*:

> It is the custom in the cider districts of Sussex to 'worsle' the apple-trees on New Year's Eve, and for several succeeding days, and it is considered unlucky to omit doing so. Farmers give a few pence to the worslers, who form a circle round the trees and sing at the top of their voices:
>
> > *Stand fast root*
> > *Bear well top,*
> > *Pray God send us*
> > *A good howling crop.*
> > *Every twig,*
> > *Apples big.*
> > *Every bough,*
> > *Apples enow,*
> > *Hats full, caps full,*
> > *Full quarter sacks full.*
> > *Holloa, boys, holla! Huzza!'*

and then all shout in chorus, with the exception of one boy who blows a loud blast on a cow's horn. Last New Year's Eve the mother of a sick boy told me that her poor child was sadly put out because he was not able to 'worsle' his grandfather's apple trees; and it is quite certain that both mother and child expected a total failure of the apple-crop in the grandfather's orchard to follow the omission.

The most famous and long standing apple-howlers in West Sussex were the Knight family of Duncton who 'worsled' the Duncton environs every Twelfth Night up until about 1923. The only known photograph of traditional apple howling in the south-east dates from about

1897 and shows the leader Richard 'Spratty' Knight the Duncton miller, his wife and his son Arthur (who led the team in its decline for a few years after the First World War). In the photo the miller is wearing a brightly patterned costume with a string of apples around his neck and a large decorated straw hat with apples round it; he is blowing a copper and brass hunting horn, which appeared in an exhibition in 1982 and was inscribed 'Thomas Bridger, Duncton Beagles, November 1860.' Mrs Knight is holding a jug of cider and a Twelfth Night cake.

Two excellent accounts survive. *The Sussex Daily News* Account of 8 January 1919 shows the custom struggling for survival, with Arthur Knight having moved out of Duncton:

> The war has done its best to kill our customs and habits, but customs die hard. And so one finds that the quaint ceremony of 'wassailing' or charming the apple trees observed at the Down village of Duncton is one which has so far survived. Nevertheless things are not as they used to be. In years gone by when the old chief, Mr Dick Knight, was alive 'wassailing' night was always a great event in the village. When the old chief died his son, Mr Arthur Knight, promised he would carry on the tradition of the village, and he has faithfully fulfilled his promise. Every year he re-visits his native village on old Christmas Eve to head the wassailers in their pilgrimage to the orchards. This year his followers numbered only three. The smallness of the band was not surprising for, as the chief remarked, 'there is no-one about now'—many 'wassailers' are engaged in sterner work than the charming of apple trees. Despite the small number of 'wassailers' and the downpour of rain, the usual visits were made to Mrs Court's, Lavington Park, Mr Seldon's, Mrs Knight, at the home of the old chief, and the mill 'neath the apple trees.

A letter in the *West Sussex Gazette* 5 January 1967 from Mr E. F. Turner of Westhampnett, the 'youngest of the family living at Mill Farm, Duncton' during the last days of the wassailing there) describes the events:

Duncton Apple Howling, *c.* 1897. (*Petworth Magazine*)

The first Captain of the Wassailers I remember was Dick Knight, who had a dark spade beard. We children would become very excited as 'Old Christmas Eve' (January 5th) got nearer, and on the night we used to be continually opening the back door to listen for the wassailers.

At last we would hear them, faintly at first and gradually getting louder. It sounded as though they split into two parties, one coming down the lane on one side of the millpond and the second through the orchard on the other. What we heard was something like this:

ALL TOGETHER: 'Here stands a good old apple tree' (or 'Nanny tree', or 'Green pippen tree', etc).
FIRST PARTY: 'Stand fast root.'
SECOND PARTY: 'Bear well top.'
FIRST PARTY: 'Every little bough.'
SECOND PARTY: 'Bear apples enow'.
FIRST PARTY: 'Every little twig'.
SECOND PARTY: 'Bear apples big.'
FIRST PARTY: 'Hat fulls
SECOND PARTY: 'Capfulls.'
FIRST PARTY: 'Three score sackfulls.'
CAPTAIN: 'Holler, boys, holler.'

Then there would be a burst of horn-blowing, shouting and a general racket. Sometimes a big bad word would float across when someone trod in a hole or tripped over a root.

When they reached the house, they would come into the big kitchen, with its pump, sink, bread-oven, three coppers and fireplace to sing songs and drink cider. One would be carrying the enormous cowhorn, and the Captain would have on a robe made of something like a flowered cretonne and a straw hat with big apples all round the wide brim, and a bow of wide ribbon.

His song was about 'Three bold fishermen rolling down the tide' and someone with 'three golden chains hanging dangling three times round.' The tune was marvellous.... I think his son sang 'Two Little Girls in Blue.'

Fred Lock from Upwaltham was a regular. He sang 'Bid Adieu to Old England'. You might get anything from John Rowe or Bernard Connor. People said they could remember enough songs to last for two hours or so. We generally had 'The Farmer's Boy', 'If I Were a Blackbird', 'Seagull' and 'Farmer Giles' among others.

My sisters used to stand near the doorway leading out of the kitchen, ready to go to the cellar for more cider or else to vanish for the time being if a song seemed to be getting salty.

When they left, we used to go outside to hear more wassailing, the voices getting fainter and fainter as they went through another part of the orchard on their way to the next stopping place.

In the course of time Dick Knight's place as Captain was taken by his son ... Arthur. I think the wassailers stopped coming in the early twenties, but in 1920 or thereabouts I heard Jack Court sing 'The Sunshine of Your Smile' and someone else, who seemed put out because he did not know any old songs, sang 'Back Home in Tennessee'.

One of the songs which Mr Turner remembers being sung at the apple wassailing is 'The Bold Fisherman'. This is a very well known folksong in Sussex and it is impossible to know which version Richard Knight sang to accompany the Duncton 'Howling'. The Sussex and

Hampshire Folk Song Collector Clive Carey collected a version from Leonard Glaysher in the village of Borden in East Hampshire in 1911. This is not far from Duncton and is therefore contemporaneous with Richard Knight's apple wassailing. It is a good example of a carol not specifically written for Christmas (it mentions May!). As it stands, the Fisherman in this carol is clearly an allegory of Christ the fisher of men gathering souls and the motif of Christ as bridegroom is one relevant for example to the condition of nuns, who regarded Christ as their lover/husband. But 'The Bold Fisherman' song has elements of a May seduction song in which it was presumably the lady who was originally laid down, rather than the 'fishing gown'! There is thus an interesting conflation of sacred and secular, of celibacy and fertility:

'The Bold Fisherman'

As I walked out one May morning,
Down by the river side,
And there I Beheld a bold fisherman
Come rowing down the tide.
Come rowing by the tide,
And there I beheld a bold fisherman
Come rowing down the tide.

'Good morning to you, bold fisherman,
How came you a-fishing here?'
'I've come a-fishing for your sweet sake,
All down this river clear.'

He rowed his boat up to the shore
And unto him this lady went,
And in taking hold of her lily-white hand
Which was his full intent.

Then he pulled off his fishing gown
And laid it on the ground,
And there she beheld three chains of gold
Came wrinkling three times round.

Then on her bended knees she fell,
And as for mercy called,
'I call-ed you a bold fisherman,
But I think you are some lord.'

'Rise up, rise up, my dear' cried he
'From off those bended knees.
There's not one word you've said or done
That has least offended me.'

Then come unto my father's house
And married we will be,
And you shall have a bold fisherman
To row you on the sea.'

The Copper Family from Rottingdean have an interesting version in 5/4 time.

Charlotte Latham mentions a variant of the Dorset belief in the kneeling of animals on Christmas Eve mentioned by Thomas Hardy: 'There is an old belief, held by many here, that on St John's Eve all the beasts of the field go down upon their knees at the hour of midnight'.

Mrs Latham also mentions the Christmas Day superstition that 'If you were born on Christmas Day, you will neither be drowned nor hanged'

New Year

At Hastings in the 1870s apples, nuts, oranges and coins were thrown from windows for fishermen and boys to scramble for them. At the Red Lion at Shoreham, in the nineteenth century, a bushel measure was filled with ale, decorated and served free of charge.

West Gallery Music

One consequence of the advent of Protestantism was that parishioners took control of the sacred music. Villagers sang and played from wooden galleries erected at the west end of churches, often performing locally written hymns and carols, to the accompaniment of fiddles, oboes, clarinets, flutes and serpents. Their Christmas music was particularly distinctive and Sussex parish choirs in the Victorian and Edwardian eras were often 'invited' (and expected) to give carol performances on Christmas Eve both at nearby great houses and at the local vicarage. They made their way there on foot, carrying their instruments, no-matter how inclement the weather, and were usually given monetary re-numeration as well as food and drink. Frederick Jones was a Sussex vicar's son and played the flute in the choir at Falmer Church and gives his boyhood memories of the Falmer and Stanmer choirs paying their annual Christmas Eve visit in 1847 in an article he contributed to *The Sussex County Magazine* in 1928; Mr Jones was then aged 86 and living in East Hoathly. The 'great house' mentioned is probably Stanmer Park:

In old days, the choirs of Stanmer and Falmer combined at the festive time, and on Christmas Eve, at the at the Earl of Chichester's invitation, were marshalled in the Baronial Hall. With their violins, clarinets, bassoons, flutes and bass-viols, assembled in a circle before the burning Yule log, they sang the old time carols in a deep bass, led by fine tenors.

My memory goes back to the third Earl of Chichester with his beautiful Countess, the sister of the hero who led the Balaclava charge. In the intervals of the songs, the tall, handsome young ladies, with their brothers home from Eton and Cambridge, supplied the singers with cake and

The Village Choir, by Thomas Webster, 1847. (*Victoria & Albert Museum*)

sparkling October ale as bright as sherry. It is difficult to say who had the greater pleasure, the hosts or the guests.

   Receiving a generous gift at parting, the minstrels then came to the old rectory, my home, and there my father assisted in the carol singing, and the whole programme had to be sung through again. The carol 'See Seraphic Throngs' (harmonised by the rector of Buxted), was a special favourite, and was usually asked for. An anthem 'Arise' with a special bass solo, was another great favourite and was generally demanded.

Michael Turner, one of the most famous and distinctive of the Sussex West Gallery musicians, wore a white smock frock with a red handkerchief, tie and breeches, plus a high beaver hat on Sundays. He was clerk and sexton of Warnham church for fifty years and died in December 1885, aged 89. The following verses are inscribed on his headstone:

> *His duty done, beneath this stone*
> *Old Michael lies at rest.*
> *His rustic rig, his song, his jig*
> *Were ever of the best.*
> *With nodding head the choir he led,*
> *That none should start too soon.*
> *The second, too, he sang full true,*
> *His viol played the tune.*

Above left: West Gallery St Nicholas Church Portslade. (*Geoff Doel*)

And when at last his age had passed
One hundred less eleven
With faithful cling to fiddle string
He sang himself to heaven.

The Victorians did not take kindly to West Gallery music and supplanted it with barrel organs, pianos and organs. The Rev. K. H. MacDermott wrote a classic book on Sussex West Gallery music, *The Church Gallery Minstrels of Old Sussex* in 1922 and this and research by Vic Gammon and performances and recordings of his Hope in the Valley Group in the late twentieth century has led to a revival, currently led by Sussex Harmony.

7

Mummers Plays and Tipteerers

'Tip-teerers' is a Sussex term, defined in the Rev. William Parish's 1875 *Dictionary of the Sussex Dialect* as 'Mummers who go round performing a sort of short play at Christmas time'. Mummers performed traditional plays at midwinter in many areas of England and hundreds of texts or fragments survive and have clearly developed through oral tradition with recognisable eighteenth and nineteenth century topical allusions added in. Their origins are controversial; some have suggested affinity with European pre-Christian ritual drama with seasonal, death and resurrection, sympathetic magic and disguise elements dominant; others have suggested an eighteenth century origin commensurate with the first recorded performances and parts of texts (though this fails to explain why the parts of all traditionally taken by men). To anyone with knowledge of the development of the English language and in particular dramatic forms, the texts, or their origin, in part clearly go back at least to the mid-sixteenth century and the crusading ethos could take us back even earlier.

The appearance of St George (who in his saint's life was resurrected) in the mummers' play hints at Christianisation of something earlier devoted to death and resurrection, though he was also the patron saint of the early crusaders. His featuring in the play is further evidence that the plays (in some form) are earlier than the seventeenth century as saints were out of favour in Protestant England. This is why in some of the plays the hero becomes King George, a change presumably made when there were four successive King Georges on the throne of Britain.

The texts of the mummer plays have that mixture of rhyme and prose and the boastful assertions found in Elizabethan and Jacobean drama. The texts are clearly influenced by popular stories of St George in circulation and in particular by Richard Johnson's prose work *The Famous Historie of the Seavern Champions of Christendom* (1596) and a blank verse stage play adapted from it by John Kirke in 1638. Both these works interacted with a succession of popular chapbooks on the life of St George. After the closure of the theatres in 1642, Kirke's play entered the puppet show repertoires and indeed Sicilian puppet shows (for example some I have seen in Syracuse) also feature boasting champions and the crusades.

Records of dozens of Sussex teams and nearly as many plays survive in Sussex, with the villages around Chichester and Midhurst forming a particularly strong tradition. The earliest account of a team of mummers in Sussex is in the Chichester area and confirms that, as in Thomas Hardy's Dorset, the actors were mainly young lads. This sad account of the inquest

Tonbridge Mummers at Bodiam Castle, 2017. (*Christine Duke*)

The Chithurst Tipteerers, 1911. (*Reading Museum of Rural Life*)

of a dead mummer from *The Hampshire Telegraph* of 31 December 1821 (kindly supplied to me by the Chichester Museum) shows the effect of excessive alcohol from the night's entertainment on a thirteen year old:

> Melancholy Circumstance which took place in Sussex on 29 December. A party of youths with a view of keeping up an old custom denominated Tip Teering sallied from Chichester on Monday evening and pursued the route of Hampnett (Westhampnett,) Welberton (Walberton) and Goodwood and having finished their tuneful sound they agreed in order to counteract the effects of the cold to run home, when Richard Cooper aged 13 years who was hindmost, having fallen in a ploughed field was left behind. On a search being made a short time afterward he was discovered lifeless in a field at Woodend. The extra beverage which he had taken combined with the cold and damp situation in which he fell caused his death. VERDICT—Died from the inclemency of the weather. (*The Hampshire Telegraph*, 31 December 1821).

Frederick Sawyer in his article 'Sussex Folk-Lore and Customs' mentions mummers still to be seen in Bramber, Shoreham, Southwick and Portslade, those in the latter calling at houses. He says mummers were also seen 'within the last twenty years' at Furze Hill in Hove.

The earliest text for a Sussex mummers' play seems to be that for Selmeston, given by W. D. Parish in his *Dictionary of Sussex Dialect*, 1875. In this play Father Christmas introduces St George, who fights against the Turkish Knight, after mutual boasting speeches, and kills him. The Doctor revives the dead knight and they fight again and the death and cure are repeated, which is very unusual. It is also unusual that in the Selmeston play, the Doctor begs for money from the audience, rather than the begging being undertaken by a walk-on character at the end, such as Johnny Jack, Beelzebub or Devil Doubt. Here the Doctor ends the play with the words:

> *Ladies and gentlemen, our play is ended,*
> *Our money-box is recommended;*
> *Copper or silver or gold if you can,*
> *Five or six shillings will do us no harm.*

Arthur Beckett in his book *The Wonderful Weald*, gives the most detailed account of performance, with the full text and details of songs. By the time that Arthur Beckett saw the Compton Mummers Play on Boxing Day 1911, photographed it and took down the text, the play was a well-established practice which gave social enjoyment and some benefit in money, food and drink. Arthur Beckett's account of the Compton play is a classic in its observation of ethos and detail:

> Among the many pleasant and delectable things of old-time Sussex there was ... a certain play or mummery, the which it was a custom to perform at the season of Christmas. This play was a rustic play, being given by villages. It was, moreover, not only ancient but curious. Also, so far as I could gather, it had not any special title; but in west Sussex the players called themselves 'Tipteerers'.
>
> I had once seen this play or mummery given when I was a boy ... Some years later I met another band of Tipteerers in a village near Worthing.... I am informed by Mr T. Fisher Unwin

that an annual performance of the Tipteerers Play has been given every Christmas for the last six or seven years by schoolboys at Mrs Fisher Unwin's country house at Heyshott (Richard Cobden's birthplace). Mrs Unwin remembers the villagers performing the play in the kitchen at 'Dunford' at Christmas in the sixties. It was also given in Lodsworth village about the same time.

Beckett's description of the Compton Tipteerers follows:

There presently came into the vicarage drive a number of young men and boys fantastically arrayed; and counting them I found that there were seven, all curiously dressed but one, who had not attempted to disguise his modern clothes. But he was not the least important personage, for he carried an accordion to play upon during the march, and a cow's horn by which he announced the coming of the Tipteerers to outlying farms and houses; also his was the hat that took largesse from the spectators such time as the play was brought to its conclusion.

Of the characters of the play I learned that these, in such sort, were named Father Christmas, St George, The Valiant Soldier, Little Johnny Jack, the Doctor and the Turk. There should have been another representing Beelzebub, but for some reason or another he did not appear, and his part was therefore taken by Father Christmas. It was well that the names of the characters were given to me, for by no indication of his dress could I have gathered the part each man was to play. Thus, Father Christmas wore an old top hat in which was a pheasant's wing and a bunch of mistletoe; his face was blacked (and in this matter of blacking the features he followed the custom that I had previously observed in other rustics who played his part); his long beard was of horsehair. He wore a long frock-coat, and, moreover, he carried a weapon which reminded me

The Compton Tipteerers, 1911. (*Arthur Beckett*)

of a Zulu's knobkerrie. Imagine him! The heathen Turk wore a policeman's or soldier's helmet (the back part turned to the front) decorated with rags of many colours. Strips of coloured rags also covered his clothes; and similar decorations were worn by the other players, some having cut out pieces of tinted cloth to represent quaint animals and figures, and some wearing a high head-gear in which they had stuck pheasant's tail feathers. Wooden staves represented swords and spears.... The actors themselves were the village smith and certain farm labourers, and each had his trousers braced high above the tops of his heavy soled boots.

The Compton Tipteerers told me that the words of their play had never been written down, but that they themselves had learnt them from predecessors, and thus the play had been handed down for hundreds of years since the time it was first written. I had some little difficulty in persuading those good fellows to commit their mummery to writing, for no single man knew the parts of his fellows; and when at length the written words were delivered to me I found the speeches strangely jumbled, rhyming lines being written as prose, no indication of the character speaking being given.... I shall ... give you the play as I disentangled it from the pencilled manuscript which ultimately came to me, correcting only certain spellings, but preserving the words as they were spoken ... being a Sussex play, it is, in certain respects, different from all others, though I doubt not it has become corrupted in its passage through the years.

Upon receiving a signal one of the Compton Tipteerers stepped a pace in front of his fellows. He represented 'The Valiant Soldier' and he delivered his speech in an even sing-song voice; in fact no sort of inflection was observed in the delivery of the lines of any character.

Despite what Arthur Beckett said about 'no single man' knowing 'the part of his fellows' Old Father Christmas did double as Beelzebub at short notice in the performance he witnessed and presumably knew the lines.

The Compton Tipteerers Play

> Valiant Soldier:
> In come I, a roamer, a gallant roamer,
> Give me room to rhyme,
> I've come to show you British sport
> Upon this Christmas time.
> Stir up your fire and give us a light,
> And see the merry actors fight.
> For in this room there shall be shown
> The heaviest battle ever known,
> Betwixt St George and the Turkish Knight.
> If you don't mind to believe these few words I've got to say,
> Let the old Gentleman of all slip in and clear the way.
>
> St George:
> In come I, St George, that man of honour and courage, stout and bold;
> With my sword and spear all by my side I have won twelve crowns of gold.

It was I who fought the Fiery Dragon and brought him to great slaughter,
And by those means I hope to win the King of Egypt's oldest daughter.

Valiant Soldier:
In come I, a soldier stout and bold;
As I was walking along the road
I heard great wonders and talks of you, St George;
If I was to meet thee I would prick thee through and through,
And make thy precious blood to flow.
Come in, thou Turkish Knight,
While we are here to-night
We are not to bear the blame.

Turkish Knight:
In come I, the Turkish Knight,
Just come from Turkey-land to fight.
I'll fight thee, St George—that man of honour, courage, stout and bold,
Let not his blood be ever so hot I will quickly make it cold.

St George (aside):
Dare say you would, too!
Stand back, stand back, you noble Turk, or by my sword you'll die,
I'll cut your giblets through and through, and make your buttons fly.

Turkish Knight:
Pardon me, St George, pardon me I crave.
And ever more will I be thy Turkish slave.

St George:
You saucy little rascal! Ask me to spare your life after being so confounded bold! Been up in my best room, and stole my best clothes! Not only that, but took a watch from my pocket. I'll up with my sword and run thee through and through.
(Does so, Turk falls).
(To Father Christmas)
Behold, old man, and see what I have done,
I've cut your noble champion down just like the evening sun.

Father Christmas:
Seems as if you have done it know.

St George:
Well Father, what was I to do? He gave me the challenge three or four times and why should I deny?

Father Christmas:
Go home, you saucy rascal! Behold, yea, is there a doctor to be found?

The Doctor (coming forward):
Yes, old Gentleman, there is a doctor to be found
Who can quickly rise your poor son who lies bleeding on the ground.

Father Christmas:
Do you call yourself a doctor?

The Doctor:
Yes, old gentleman, I am a doctor.

Father Christmas:
You comes in more like three-ha'porth o' bad luck than you do a doctor.

The Doctor:
Don't matter what I come in like, or what I look like, as long as I can rise your poor son
who lies bleeding on the ground.

Father Christmas:
I don't know as you can do it yet. What is your pay?

The Doctor:
Ten pound is my pay;
Full fifty I'll have out of you before you go away,
You not being a poor man.

Father Christmas:
I can't pay so much money as that;
I'd sooner let him lay there and die.

The Doctor:
Stop, old gentleman, I'll satisfy you with quarter-part o' that.

Father Christmas:
That's according to what you can cure.

The Doctor:
I can cure all sorts of diseases:
The itch, the stick, the palsy, the gout,
Raging pains within and without.
This young man's arm's broke, his leg's broke,
Calf swollen up as big as a tan-leather bottle.

Father Christmas:
As big as a wooden-legged bottle, more like it.

The Doctor:
Rec'lect. old gentleman, I an't been about all my time a-life without knowing nothing.

Father Christmas:
Where did you get all your learning from?

The Doctor:
I travelled for it: I travelled France, 'Merica, Spain and Dover,
I travelled the wide world all over.
I served my 'prenticeship in St John's Hospital seven year all one summer.

Father Christmas:
Seven year all one winter, more like it.

The Doctor:
I could rise this young man before your face. So could you if you know'd how and which way. So I did and so I can. I rose my poor old grandmother after she had been dead a hundred and ninety-nine years. She cut her throat with a ball o' rice; I slipt in and sewed it up with a rice-chain.

Father Christmas:
Talk about what you run-about doctors can do!

The Doctor:
Look here, old gentleman. I had a man brought to me the other day; indeed, he was not brought to me, he was wheeled to me in a left-handed wheel-barrow. He could not see anything without opening his eyes, and could not speak without moving his tongue.

Father Christmas (aside):
(No) more would you,
Or else you would not talk so fast as you do.

The Doctor:
Look about, old gentleman, another curious trick I'll show you before I go away. Look deedy, or else you won't see it kick, and troublesome cure yourself for me.
(Going).

Father Christmas:
Stop, doctor, stop! Come and try one of your pills on my poor son, sooner than having him lying about here all this Christmas.

The Doctor:
I've got a little bottle in my waistcoat trouser breeches pocket, what they call *okum,*
slokum, elegant plaint. I don't.

Father Christmas:
What do you call it?

The Doctor:
That makes no difference, so long as you drop
One drop on the young man's heart and another on his brain,
He will rise and fight bold Champion again.
(Doctor proceeds to cure Turk.)

Turkish Knight:
How long have I been lying on this floor?
Ten minutes or more,
I've been urged and scourged and dragged from door to door.
To-morrow morning at the hour of five,
I'll meet thee, St George, if I am alive.

St George:
To-morrow morning, at the hour of ten,
I'll meet thee spring guard, with fifty thousand men.
I'll hage thee, gage thee, and let thee know
That I am St George over old England.
Go home, go home, you Turkish Knight,
Go home to your country and fight;
And tell those 'Mericans what I've done;
I've killed ten thousand to thy one.
Now I am off (to) my discharge.
God bless the Turk, likewise St George.

Johnny Jack:
In come I, little Johnny Jack,
Wife and family at my back.
Though I am so little and small
I am the biggest rogue among you all.
If any man offend me I bring him to a stand.
Cutter and Slasher is my name,
From those blessed wars I came.
It was only me and seven more
Fought the battle of a score,
And boarded a man-of-war.

Cut them up as fine as any flying dust,
Send them to cook-shop to make mince-pie crust.

St George:
What little rattling, prattling tongue is that I hear?

Johnny Jack:
That's mine, sir.

St George:
If I hear any more of that, you and me will have a cut before we part'
On my heart, before we part.

Turkish Knight:
In come I, Cuts and Scars,
Just returning from those wars.
Many a battle I've been in,
Many a battle I have seen.
I've seen St George and all his royal men.
Cannon ball passed by my head with spite—
I lost my height.
Twice through the head I've been shot,
Which makes my brain boil like my old pot.
What more can be bolder?
Enter in the Valiant Soldier.

Valiant Soldier:
In come I, a Valiant Soldier, Bold and Slasher is my name,
With my sword and spear all by my side I hope to win this game.
Now I am a soldier stout and bold,
I make many a man's blood run cold.
Now I am returning from those wars,
I am a man like you, full of cuts and scars.
Pull out your sword and fight, pull out your purse and pay,
Satisfaction I will have before I go away.

Turkish Knight:
No satisfaction will I give thee, no more will I pay,
But this battle we will fight both manfully before we go away.

(They fight and are separated by Johnny Jack, alias Twin-Twan).

Johnny Jack (as Twin-Twan):
In come I, Twin-Twan,
The left hand of this press-gang;
I pressed all these bold mummers sin'
The time the ship-of-war came in.
Although my name is Saucy Jack,
Wife and family at my back,
Out of eight I've got but five,
And they are almost starved alive.
Some in the workhouse all alone,
And these at my back must be helped before I get home.
So if any man would like to fight let him come on;
I urge him, scourge him, fight him with spite,
And after that I fight the best man under the sky.

Father Christmas:
You saucy little rascal! Challenge your poor old father and all the sons he's got?

Johnny Jack:
Yes; I urge him, scourge him, fight him with spite,
And after that I fight the best man under the sky.

Beelzebub:
In come I, old Belsey Bob,
On my shoulders I carry my nob,
In my hand a dripping pan,
Don't you think I'm a funny old man?
Christmas comes but once a year,
And likes to give you jolly good cheer;
Plum-pudding, roast beef—who likes that better than anybody else?
To-night I'd like a glass of grog; a glass of beer'll suit these chaps to-night.
Price, sir! Price, sir! Give you a bit of a rub?
A halfpenny towards the rent, and a penny towards the grub.
Price, sir! Price sir! And my old bell shall ring,
Put what you like in my old hat and then these chaps will sing.

Immediately the Tipteerers joined in singing the mummers' carol:

> *As we come out on a Christmas Day,*
> *Christmas Day, Christmas Day,*
> *As we come out on a Christmas Day*
> *So early in the morning.*

We saw three ships come sailing by,
Come sailing by, come sailing by,
We saw three ships come sailing by
On Christmas Day in the morning.

And who should be in those three ships,
Those three ships, those three ships?
And who should be in those three ships?
'Twas Joseph and his Fair Lady.

He did whistle and she did sing,
And all the bells on earth did ring,
For Christ our Saviour he was born
On Christmas Day in the morning.

Jack was nimble and Jack was quick,
Jack jumped over the candlestick;
Jack was nimble and Jack was quick
On Christmas Day in the morning.

The Tipteerers then followed this with a local carol, 'Brave Joseph and Mary', received their largesse, and ended with the well known folk carol 'God Bless the Master', which thanks all in the house and gives them a blessing:

God bless the Master of this house
And send him long to reign,
And many a Merry Christmas may
He live to see again,
May he live to see again.

God bless the Mistress of this house
With a gold chain round her breast,
Where'er her body wakes or sleeps,
Lord send her soul to rest,
Lord send her soul to rest.

No mortal man can remember well
When Christ he was first born;
He was crucified between the thieves,
And crowned with those thorns,
And crowned with those thorns.

No mortal man can remember well
When Christ was on the rood;

And for our sins and wickedness
He shed his precious blood,
He shed his precious blood.

No mortal man can remember well
Where Christ was laid in clay;
He was buried in some sepulchre,
Where never no man lay,
Where never no man lay.

God bless your house, and your cattle, too
Your family and your store,
May the Lord increase them day by day,
And send you more and more,
And send you more and more.

My song is sung and I must be gone,
No longer can I stay here,
So God bless you all, both great and small
And send you a happy New Year,
Lord send you a happy new Year.

There was a large group of about twenty Tipteerers at Bosham in the late nineteenth century who acted, danced and sang each Boxing Day. They wore smocks and 'chummies', which were round black felt hats. They began at about 9 a.m. and decorated farm carts for Shopwyke House, where they were entertained. They also visited Chichester and ended their mumming about 9 p.m. There was a play at Newdigate, last performed in 1850, for which no text survives. Lucy Broadwood noted the Rusper play, which she called 'St George, the Turk, and the Seven Champions of Christendom' at Lyne in 1880 or 1881.

Other East Sussex teams and texts collected include Ovingdean, Hastings, Firle, Crowhurst and Rottingdean. By 1911 traditional customs and songs were already in decline amongst the rural working classes (themselves a diminishing sector), but fortunately the customs (including the mummers' plays) and the songs were being collected and researched. So although the First World War virtually ended the traditional performances of plays by village communities through oral transmission, the wealth of revivals by groups such as the Boxgrove Tipteers (a touring group using amalgams of traditional West Sussex texts) and the Ditchling Players between the wars and by Morris sides (notably Chanctonbury and Broadwood) and folk clubs (notably Lewes) after the Second World War has meant that not a year went by in the twentieth century without the performance of a Christmas mummers' play in Sussex, possibly a unique situation amongst counties.

There have been a considerable number of revivals of Sussex mummers' plays in the twentieth and twenty-first centuries. One of the first was the revival of the East Preston

Play by Mr Foard in 1911, which is described in an article in *The Sussex County Magazine* in 1931 by R. J. Sharp who revived the play after the First World War and organised the Boxgrove Tipteerers. In 1911, when living at East Preston, near Littlehampton, one of the villagers (a Mr Foard), revived the 'Tipteers'. As a boy he used to go round, with other boys, at the instigation of a very old man who kept a small sweet shop: the old rogue used to take the money collected and give the boys a few sweets. Foard was then some forty years old and the old man about 70.

> I … got the Iping version from a Mr Dawtrey…, using the East Preston version as a basis and the Iping for filling in. I made a complete version which was done by the East Preston men the next year at many country houses, and in 1913 at Brighton also, at the Aquarium and Royal York and Albion hotels. Removing to Chichester, I found a band of men at Boxgrove keen on preserving this old country custom, and we have kept it going since … in pre-war days the 'Tipteers' were quite a Christmas institution at all the large houses.
>
> To the Play we have added one of the few surviving old Sussex dances, 'Over the Sticks', a species of sword dance done over crossed flails. Our Doctor's Top Hat and Noble Captain's sword were used by the East Marden Tipteers over 70 years ago.

R. J. Sharp lamented the decline of the great country estates, which he regarded as an essential setting for the plays in Sussex. There are records of a considerable number of teams and plays in the Chichester area: Angmering, Midhurst, East Preston, West Stoke, Iping (for which a complete text survives), East Marden, West Wittering (for which a text survives), Cocking (the play collected by Reginald Tiddy), Westbourne and Ferring. The Chithurst Tipteerers were photographed in 1911 and the play collected by Dorothy Marshall, who lived at Chithurst House. There were seven 'champions'—Father Christmas with a holly bush on a staff; Jolly John (or Jack); the Gallant Soldier dressed in a military uniform with medals; King George the Fourth; The Turkish Knight; The Noble Captain and Doctor Good. Most wore tunics covered with coloured strips of cloth hanging like ribbons. Their hats were decorated with streamers and flowers.

Tony Wales researched further details of the East Preston tradition—that Mr Foard was a farmhand and that as a boy he was in a gang of tipteerers led by an old man named Barnard who took the part of Father Christmas and who also organised the boys to take a guy round on November the Fifth, keeping the money from that too. R. J. Sharp was a fiddle player and the Boxgrove Tipteers met once a week at his instigation to rehearse the play and sing Sussex songs, including 'The Jolly Woodcutter' and 'The Littlehampton Collier'. The Boxgrove Tipteerers were photographed at the Anglesey Arms, Halnaker in 1936 by the well-known photographer George Garland and there are half a dozen photos in the Garland Collection at the West Sussex Record Office in Chichester. In January 1937 they performed at the Festival of English Folk-Song and Dance at the Albert Hall. A Sussex newspaper account of 1938 mentions that the Boxgrove Tipteers were in their twelfth year of revival, but it was terminated by the Second World War. The characters in their play were: Father Christmas, Noble Captain, St George, Prince of Peace, Turkish Knight, Valiant Soldier, Doctor, and Little Jolly Jack, a popular begging figure in many of the Sussex plays, who ends the play with the lines:

In comes I, Little Jolly Jack,
My wife and family all upon my back.
Though my family be but small,
I can scarce find bread and cheese for them all.
Christmas comes but once a year
And when it comes it brings good cheer.
Roast beef, plum pudding and mince pie,
Who likes these any better than I?
Christmas fare makes us dance and sing,
Money in the purse is a capital thing.
Ladies and gentlemen give what you please,
Old Father Christmas will welcolmely receive.

Little Jolly Jack carried dolls on his back to represent his impoverished family; Mr Sharp played the fiddle at the play.

The Fittleworth mummers' play was revived in the 1930s, with traditional singer George Attrill, who had taken part in the play as a boy, playing Father Christmas. The play was further revived in 1945. After the introductory speech by Father Christmas, a character called 'Billy Twing Twang' comes in, connected with the Press Gang, and found in several Sussex mummers' plays. After a skirmish between King George and the Turkish Knight, the Valiant Soldier then fights on behalf of King George; the poetic and evocative lines: 'I've cut him down like the evening sun' are also found in some other West Sussex plays. After the death of the combatant and the revival by the Doctor, the Prince of Peace bids 'all these awful wars to cease'.

The Second Folk Revival of the 1960s and 1970s was particularly strong in Sussex and I saw my first mummers' play in 1965 at Steyning, a version of the Steyning Play performed by the Chanctonbury Morris Men, complete with dragon. The Broadwood Morris Men perform a play collected by Lucy Broadwood from Lyne House, Rusper, from the local tipteerers in 1880 or 1881, who 'clustered together, wooden swords in hand, at the close of their play 'St George and the Turk' and sang… they wore dresses of coloured calico, heavily trimmed with shreds of ribbon, gaudy paper fringes and odd ornaments.'

Vic & Tina Smith revived the Chithurst Play at the Lewes Folk Club in the 1970s and my own side, the Tonbridge Mummers and Hoodeners, have revived several Sussex Plays, including Compton, Cocking and Iping. The Copper family have revived one of the Rottingdean plays and Clive Bennett's Merrie England Mummers revived the Firle Play, which is also performed by the Hartley Morris at Wrotham in Kent on Boxing Day. The Tonbridge Mummers have recently (up to 2017) been performing at Sussex National Trust properties in December, such as Batemans and Bodiam Castle.

8

Renewal:
Spring and Summer Customs

St Valentine's Day

Traditionally spring begins on St Valentine's Day (14 February) when the birds mate—'the Birds' Wedding Day' as it was called in Sussex. Geoffrey Chaucer uses this tradition in his dream-vision poem 'The Parliament of Fowls' (*c.* 1382):

> *For this was on seynt Valentynes day,*
> *Whan every foul cometh there to chese his make,*
> *Of every kynde that men thynke may.*

That sexual pairing on this day extended to human beings, at least symbolically and traditionally, is shown by the final verse of the folksong 'Dame Durden', found extensively in the south of England including in the repertoire of the famous Copper Family from Rottingdean:

> *Dame Durden kept five servant maids to carry the milking pail,*
> *She also kept five labouring men to use the spade and flail.*
>
> *Chor: Twas Moll & Bet & Doll & Kit & Dorothy Draggletail,*
> *It was Tom & Dick & Joe & Jack & Humphrey with his flail.*
> *Then Tom kissed Molly and Dick kissed Betty*
> *And Joe kissed Dolly and Jack kissed Kitty*
> *And Humphrey with his flail.*
> *And Kitty she was a charming maid to carry the milking pail.*
>
> *Dame Durden in the morn so soon, she did begin to call,*
> *To rouse her servants, maids and men she did begin to bawl.*
>
> *''Twas on the morn of Valentine when birds began to prate*
> *Dame Durden and her maids and men they altogether mate.*

The song probably originated on the London stage at the end of the seventeenth century. The Copper family version bowdlerises the sexual word 'mate' to 'meet'.

In the seventeenth and eighteenth centuries there was a custom that the first man to greet a lady on St Valentine's Day would be her valentine; husbands apparently didn't count! This involved the man buying the lady a present, such as a pair of gloves and some harmless social contact later in the day (such as sitting next to each other at a Valentine Day's feast); probably a kiss was also permitted. That the lady had to 'accept' the first comer, and therefore contrived to ensure the man was acceptable, is shown by the reference in *Samuel Pepys' Diary* for St Valentine's Day 1662:

> Valentine's day. I did this day purposely shun to be seen at Sir W. Battens—because I would not have his daughter to be my Valentine, as she was the last year, there being no great friendship between us now as formerly. This morning in comes W. Bowyer, who was my wife's Valentine, she having (at which I made good sport to myself) held her hands all the morning, that she might not see the paynters that were at work in gilding my chimney-piece and pictures in my dining-room.

Originally gifts were sent to one's Valentine; there are records of this happening in Roman society at this time of year and the festival, named after an early Christian martyr, may have absorbed features of some earlier celebration or ritual connected with spring-time courtship. In the eighteenth century love messages were sent and in the nineteenth century, Valentine cards. Shakespeare has a hero called Valentine who serenades his love outside her bedroom window in his play *The Two Gentlemen of Verona* and in East Anglia there are records of children singing love songs outside houses on Valentine's morn to collect pennies, which might be the remnants of an adult custom.

Shrovetide

Shrovetide is a moveable spring festival; the name derives from two Anglo-Saxon words meaning 'the time to be shriven'—to confess one's sins before the forty day Lenten fast during which the consuming of meat, milk, eggs, butter and cheese were forbidden on weekdays. In pre-Reformation days, after a church service and shrivings there was the consumption of food forbidden in Lent incorporated into traditional pancakes to be used up and then the playing of rough sports unsuitable for Lent, such as cock-fighting, played in the Brighton lanes up until 1780 on Shrove Tuesday. The pancakes and violent sports survived the Reformation. The Sussex folklorist Tony Wales has drawn attention to the popularity of cock throwing at Billingshurst in the later eighteenth century and how a Unitarian minister there helped its demise by pinning poem 'The Cock's Remonstrance on Shrove Tuesday' to his church door. The *Lewes Journal* proclaimed in 1778:

> It is with great pleasure we can inform the public that the barbarous practice of throwing at cocks is now so universally exploded in these parts that Shrove Tuesday did not produce a single instance of those acts of riot and cruelty by which this day was long and shamefully characterized, in open defiance of humanity and all civil authority.

The Reverend Giles Moore noted in his Journal in 1656: 'I received of Thomas Morley for 6 cocks which I sold him at Shrove Tide, 4s. 6d.' But there was also cock fighting at other times of the year. Thomas Turner has two references to cock fighting in his diary:

June 10, 1761—Was fought this day, at Jones's, a main of cocks, between the gentlemen of Hothley and Pevensey.

May 2 1764—This day was fought a main of cocks, at our public-house, between the gentlemen of East Grinstead and the gentlemen of East Hothley, for half-a-guinea a battle and two guineas the odd battle, which was won by the gentlemen of East Grinstead, they winning five battles out of six fought in the main. I believe there was a deal of money sported on both sides.

Heffle (Heathfield) Cuckoo Fair

In Sussex the belief is that spring starts at Heffle (Heathfield) Cuckoo Fair on 14 April, when an old woman lets a cuckoo out of a bag. This is celebrated in a famous poem by Rudyard Kipling:

'Heffle Cuckoo Fair'

Tell it to the locked-up trees,
Cuckoo, bring your song here!
Warrant, Act and Summons, please,
For Spring to pass along here!
Tell old Winter, if he doubt,
Tell him squat and square-a!
Old Woman!
Old Woman!
Old Woman's let the Cuckoo out
At Heffle Cuckoo Fair-a!

March has searched and April tried—
'Tisn't long to May now.
Not so far to Whitsuntide,
And Cuckoo's come to stay now!
Hear the valiant fellow shout
Down the orchard bare-a!
Old Woman!
Old Woman!
Old Woman's let the Cuckoo out
At Heffle Cuckoo Fair-a!

When your heart is young and gay
And the season rules it—
Work your works and play your play
'Fore the Autumn cools it!

Kiss you turn and turn about,
But my lad, beware-a!
Old Woman!
Old Woman!
Old Woman's let the Cuckoo out
At Heffle Cuckoo Fair-a

Charlotte Latham also refers to this tradition:

A certain old woman of irascible temper has charge of all the cuckoos, and that in the spring she fills her apron with them, and if she is in a good humour, allows several to take flight, but only permits one or two to escape if anything has happened to sour her temper.

Lent

Marble playing, as a quiet game, was encouraged during Lent in Sussex in the nineteenth century up until the 1950s, culminating on Good Friday. The nineteenth century antiquarian Rev. Parish comments:

In the country districts in Sussex the marble season is strictly defined between Ash Wednesday and Good Friday, and on the last day of the season it seems to be the object of every man and boy to play marbles as much as possible. They will play in the road at the church gate till the last moment before service, and begin again the instant they are out of church. Persons play at

Marble Playing in Lent at West Chiltington. (*Tony Wales Collection*)

marbles on Good Friday who would never think of playing on any other day. Is it possible that it was appointed a Lenten sport, to keep people from more boisterous and mischievous enjoyments?

I think Rev. Parish is correct in his surmises, especially as 'boisterous and mischievous enjoyments' framed the austere Lenten period on Shrove Tuesday and Easter Monday in many parts of the county. Frederick Sawyer writes in 1883 that he had previously been told by James Rolf, 'an old Brighton fisherman' that Brighton fishermen used to commence playing marbles on Ash Wednesday and continue through Lent to Good Friday. He also mentioned Cuckfield as a strong area for playing marbles. Marble playing on Good Friday is recorded in St Leonard's Churchyard, Seaford.

A whole technical vocabulary for the playing of marbles exists in Sussex dialect; some of the terms have taken on a wider currency, for example 'inching', defined by the *Dictionary of Sussex Dialect* as: 'The practice of the privilege a shooter at marbles has of approaching with his hands the target so that the shot is less in length: sometimes only a span'.

Nowadays competitive marble playing survives only in pockets. At Battle where the tolley or shooting marble is known as a 'bosser' and in the area around Gatwick Airport there are marble-rinks outside pubs in Charlwood, Turner's Hill and a few other nearby villages. But the centre of the marble-playing world is Tinsley Green, where the Greyhound Inn has hosted the British and World Marbles Championship on Good Friday since 1932, when the event was founded by an enthusiast from nearby Horley. Sam Spooner is commemorated by a plaque outside the pub; he took part in the 1932 championship using the same shooting marble, or 'tolley' that he had used as a marbles player in the 1880s. Among the early champions (and eventually captain of the England team) was George 'Pop' Maynard, whose family team won the cup several times in the 1940s.

Modern teams often carry graphic names like the 'Tinsley Tigers', The 'Handcross Rebels', 'The Hirst Horribles', the 'Moonshiners', the 'Turner's Hill Tolleymen and 'The Copthorne Cherypickers'. A ladies' team is called the 'Bakewell Tarts'. The 'Black Dog Boozers' were champions in 1994 and the 'Barrel Scrapers' in 1995. Championship marbles, 'Ring Taw', is a more complex game than the schoolboy version and might be compared to outdoor snooker. It has been suggested that it was originally played in church porches by men waiting for the Good Friday service to begin. A circle of forty nine marbles is set down in the middle of a sanded ring, six feet in diameter. Teams of six, each with his or her own tolley (shooting marble), try to knock these marbles from the ring; the tolleys are flicked by the thumb from a crooked index-finger. Pushing, or 'fudging', is against the rules, which are strictly applied by a referee. The first team to dislodge twenty five marbles is the winner. If a player's tolley ends in the ring without knocking a marble out, it must stay there until the player's next shot and if it is knocked out before then he is 'killed' and can take no further part.

The Rev. Parish records another variant of the Sussex game of marbles known as 'Bigoring':

A marbles game where the players contribute equally to the pool of marbles placed in the middle of a ring 3 feet or so in diameter, and shoot in turns from the circumference. If the player knock out one or more marbles they are his spoil, and he can go on so long as he remains in the ring and gets one or more marbles out at each shot. If he remain in and fail to get a marble out he becomes dead and can be shot at by the others. Also called 'Shoot-through-the-ring'.

Good Friday Marbles at Battle, 1949.

George 'Pop' Maynard and his sons playing marbles at Tinsley Green.

Good Friday Skipping

In Brighton, as in many other coastal communities, the fishermen did not go out to sea on Good Friday out of respect for Christ. Instead they organised long rope skipping, using their long and thick fishing ropes; in Brighton, Good Friday was sometimes called 'Long Rope Day'. Those wishing to give the custom a Christian significance pointed out that Judas hanged himself with a rope. The Rev. Parish records the nineteenth century custom:

> On Good Friday it is the custom of the Brighton fishermen to skip in the fish market. A rope is swung by two men and all and sundry are expected to run in and skip. Formerly every street had its own long rope. The practice is said to have a religious origin, the rope representing the one with which Judas hanged himself. The Priory of St Bartholomew (in Brighton) is known to have encouraged it.

A correspondent to *Notes and Queries*, mentioning 1863, says:

> In Brighton on this day (Good Friday) children in the back streets bring up ropes from the beach. One stands on the pavement on one side, and one on the other, while one skips in the middle of the street. Sometimes a pair (a boy and a girl) skip together, and sometimes a great fat bathing-woman will take her place, and skip as merrily as the grandsire danced in Goldsmith's 'Traveller'. They call the day 'Long Rope Day'.

'Long line Day' was another name for it. Frederick Sawyer records 'scores of skippers' on the Level at Brighton on Good Friday 1883. My mother, Olive Doel remembered and took part in Good Friday skipping in the 1920s in Brighton:

> As a girl my parents ran the Queensbury Arms (also known locally as 'the Hole in the Wall') just off Brighton seafront. On Good Friday morning I used to cross over to the fisherman's market or hard between the piers and join in the skipping. The fishermen twirled two long ropes in different directions and we used to try to jump over one without being hit by the other. The ropes were very heavy and could give you a nasty whack.

The custom ceased at Brighton at the beginning of the Second World War, when Brighton seafront was fortified, but moved for a number of years inland to the Rose Cottage Inn at Alciston, where it survived until the 1960s. It was revived again and combined with garland dancing from the Knots of May Ladies Morris team and at the time of writing (2019) is still going strong, moving to the Ram Inn at Firle. Good Friday long rope skipping at Brighton has also been revived by Andrew Duncan, whose grandmother was involved in it in the 1920s and 1930s.

Much earlier, in the 1850s, there are records of Good Friday celebrations of 'Kissing in the Ring' on a large Bronze Age tumulus in Hove, possibly the only one on the coastal plain. It was about 15 to 20 feet in height and about 200 feet in circumference. It was destroyed in 1857/8 and its site lies under the back garden of number 13 Palmeira Avenue. Some of the earth was used for making the mound of the Floral Clock in nearby Palmeira Square. In the burial mound was found the famous bronze age Amber Cup and in an article in the *Sussex*

Above left: Skipping at Brighton on Good Friday, *c.* 1937-9.

Above right: Alciston Good Friday Skipping, 2014. (*Geoff Doel*)

Hove Barrow and Tumulus, 1821. (*Drawing by Rev J. Skinner*)

Archaeological Collections of 1848, Barclay Phillips describes the excavation of the tumulus and artefacts and also briefly records the custom, which seems to have ended shortly earlier:

> Between (Brighton) and the village of Hove have existed till within the last few years, some remarkably level fields devoted to pasturage and the cultivation of grass for hay. Nearly in the centre of one of these fields ... once stood a small hillock about fifteen or twenty feet high, on the north of the pathway leading from Brighton to Hove Church, and situated about 100 yards N.N.E. of the new church of St John the Baptist; and till very lately, famous every Good Friday as the resort of hundred of young persons of both sexes to join in the rustic game of 'kiss in the ring'. Rising from a dead flat, and being unconnected with any other hills, this hillock always presented the appearance of an artificial mound.

The youngsters are said to have chanted 'Hey diddle derry, let's dance on the Bury.' Rev. Parish mentions in his book on Sussex dialect: 'There is a tradition that the sun dances on the morning of Holy Sunday, but nobody has ever seen it because the devil is so cunning that he always puts a hill in the way to hide it'.

There does seem to be a strange desire in custom to go to high places at Easter or to jump high, which perhaps relates to early superstition which has been partly adapted to Christianity. There is a Good Friday Hill in Shoreham; the name is said to derive from the custom of rolling painted hard-boiled eggs down the hill behind the church on Good Friday.

Hot Cross Buns

Frederick Sawyer comments on the importance of hot cross buns in Sussex as good luck bringers:

> Good Friday. It is almost a religious duty in Sussex to eat buns on this day, whilst buns are kept until the next Good Friday for luck, being preserved in tin boxes. A Brighton baker has informed me, that a local undertaker (lately deceased) always kept a cross bun by him, replacing the old by a new one each Good Friday. Mr Henderson (author of *Folk Lore of the Northern Counties*) says that they have been hung up in Sussex cottages, and when any illness broke out in the family, a fragment is cut off, pounded, and given as medicine! I am also informed (by Mr. John Sawyer) that to keep a cross-bun in the house is thought by some Sussex folks a preservative against fire. My informant was shown a cross-bun perfectly white from keeping, and was triumphantly told by an aged lady, the possessor, that she had never been burnt out during all the years she had kept it. The buns are sold early in the morning, the vendors shouting in the streets:

> *Hot cross buns! Hot cross buns!*
> *One a penny, two for twopence, Hot cross buns,*
> *All hot! All hot! All hot!*

In some cases in the second line they say 'Two a penny', the latter buns being of a smaller size and another variant is:

> *If your daughters do not like them,*
> *Give them to your sons*

Bread baked on this day is supposed not to turn mouldy, and Sussex country people bake small cakes or loaves for their children, though perhaps superstition is assisted to some extent by baking the cakes until they are hard.

Other sports featured on Good Friday included skittles on the Level in Brighton and egg or orange rolling at Shoreham.

May Garlands & Maypoles

May customs frequently celebrate the arrival of summer and the burgeoning of nature. Until the end of the nineteenth century, 1 May was an unofficial holiday and in the morning in Sussex, as elsewhere in the southern counties and the Midlands, children carried round May garlands. In 1771 several little girls carried their garlands to the prince of Mecklenburg-Strelitz, who was staying in Brighton, and he gave them each half a crown.

Henry Burstow describes May day and the parading of garlands in Horsham in the nineteenth century; he was born in 1826:

> May Day, or Garland Day, was a very jolly time for us youngsters, not only because it was a holiday, but also because we used to pick up what seemed to us quite a lot of money. Early in the morning we used to get up our best nosegays and garlands, some mounted on poles, and visit the private residents and tradespeople. We represented a recognised institution, and invariably got well received and patronised. People all seemed please to see us, and we were all pleased to see one another, especially if the weather was fine, as it now seems to me it always was.

Above left: Children with May Garlands at Cowfold in 1910.

Above right: Children with May Garlands at Horsham.

At Manor House special arrangements were made for our reception, and quite a delightful old-time ceremony took place. Boys and girls gaily decked out for the occasion, a few at a time, used to approach the front door, where a temporary railed platform was erected, and there old Mrs Tredcroft, a nice-looking, good-hearted old lady, used to stand and deal out to each and every one of us kind words and a few pence, everyone curtseying upon approach and on leaving.

Old Mrs Smallwood, who lived in a quaint old cottage in the Bishopric, always used to go round on May Day with an immense garland drawn on a trolley by two or three boys. On top of her garland she used to mount her little model cow, indicative of her trade –milk selling. Gaily dressed up herself in bows and ribbons, she used to take her garland all round the town, call upon all the principal residents.

An article in the *Sussex County Magazine*, 1933 'Chichester Fifty Years Ago' says that 'On May Day, the school children brought round garlands of wild flowers from door to door, singing: 'The First of May is Garland Day' and adds that the custom is to give a penny or a half penny for the most artistic production'

At Petworth the children sang as they carried round their garlands:

> *The first of May is Garland Day,*
> *So please remember the garland,*
> *We don't come here but once a year,*
> *So please remember the Garland.*

The Sussex folklorist Lilian Candlin recalls that her mother, born in 1870 in Lewes:

Went early to the Daisy Bank—a grassy slope opposite the old Fox Inn at Southeram, on the 1st May to gather wild flowers... The flowers were made into a garland which she took around to the neighbours who gave her a penny or a cake for the sight of it.

At Shoreham festivities began early in the morning with dancing and for many years it was traditional to 'knock up' local dignitaries as a beginning to May morning.

Maypoles were generally banned in the Puritan period, but made something of a comeback, though writing in about 1860, M. A. Lower notes a decline:

The observance of May-Day has become here, as elsewhere, nearly obsolete. The may-pole on the village green belongs to the past. Within the last thirty years, many a wayside inn had a tall one, crowned with a large birch broom, before its door; but such a thing is now rarely seen.

In later Victorian times, encouraged by the 'Merrie England' movement, maypoles had another revival, especially at fetes and in schools. Lucy Baldwin (wife of the prime minster) remembered the Rottingdean celebrations at the end of the nineteenth century:

On the first of May I remember a Maypole and the children dancing round it on the village green. The pole had a bunch of flowers on the top and... streamers coming from it. The custom has now died out, but later the children would bring round small posies, sing their little song and then violently ring your front door bell. The song ran as follows:

Gathering wild flowers for May Garlands near Brighton, 1936.

Battle Abbey May Carnival.

Dancing round the Maypole, Petworth Rectory Fete, 1900. Town Band in background.

> '*First of May, My birthday.*
> *Give us all A 'oliday.'*

They were quite content with a couple of pennies, but other small parties would come round in such numbers that it called forth a protest from the village school-master, with a request that no money should be given before 12, when the children came out of school.

The vicar of East Blatchington, Robert Dennis, recorded in his diary for 1 May 1850: 'Children came garlanding. Jane Mace and Phoebe Pelham had the best garland'. At Ferring, May Day was 'Garland Day' and there are late nineteenth century accounts of Ferring children going around the village showing their garlands of flowers and asking for pennies. In the 1880s George Charles arrived at school 'noisy and almost intoxicated', as he had spent money collected by showing his garland on beer! On 2 May 1881 the Logbook Southwick Board School for Girls recorded: 'several children absent carrying garlands and flowers'.

Because children played truant from school to 'go garlanding' with the ending of the unofficial May Day bank holiday in the 1880s with stricter attitudes from employers and compulsory school attendance, some schools introduced their own May revels, John Ruskin is credited with introducing a May Queen at Whitelands Teacher Training College, which subsequently encouraged the reintroduction of the May Queen in schools and villages through teachers. Ruskin also introduced, through teachers, the idea of portable maypoles and plaited maypole dancing holding streamers, which he had noticed in Europe. This largely replaced the traditional English maypole, so well described in Thomas Hardy's novel *The Return of the Native* of crossbeams with garlands and adults dancing in couples.

Adult workers sometimes featured garlands on May Day in their occupations. For example

Children and Maypole, St Michael's School, Portslade, *c.* 1911.

May Revels, Stanford School, Brighton, 1920.

Sompting May Day
Procession, 1908. (*Geoff
Doel*)

Sussex shepherds sometimes garlanded their sheep and Frederick Sawyer, writing in 1883 describes the Sussex fishermen decorating their boats on May Day:

> This day is known in Sussex as Garland Day, and is a favourite day with the Brighton fishermen for commencing mackerel fishing. When the fishermen start on this day, they decorate the masts of their boats with 'garlands', while at other times they used to accompany the sweeps in their celebration of the day.

Jack in the Greens

Jack in the Greens may have partly replaced maypoles when the latter were banned, and they had the advantage of being moveable, being a man in a wicker frame stuffed with evergreens. The custom is first recorded in London where the chimney sweeps adopted it as their form of May garland and danced around it with their brooms and shovels and featured Lord of the May, often in military costume and a male Maid Marion in the sixteenth century tradition. Why the chimney sweeps chose the Jack-in-the-Green as their garland in unknown, but the use of the term 'Jack' (as in Jack o Lent and Jack Frost and Jack o Lantern) suggests it is older than the first printed reference so far discovered in 1795. The sweeps collected money for a feast and to buy clothes for the climbing boys. As sweeps moved out of London, they took the custom with them to towns such a Horsham, Crawley, Lewes, Henfield, Brighton and Hastings. Henry Burstow saw Jack-in-the-Greens at Horsham as a boy:

> On this day, too, we had Jacks-in-the-Green. The chimney-sweeps used to dress up in fancy costumes and in evergreens and flowers, and, accompanied by a fiddler or two, parade and dance all round the town and neighbourhood. There were two sets of Jacks-in-the Green when I was a boy, the Potter and the Whiting parties, and considerable rivalry existed between them. Lady Shelley used to patronise them handsomely, giving them plenty to eat and drink, and a good round sum of money. One year she

Hastings Jack in the Green 2014. (*Geoff Doel*)

gave the Whiting party a set of new dresses, fitting them out in a very gay manner. The children with their flowers and garlands finished their part of the proceedings about noon, but the Merry Andrew parties kept the game going all day, getting merrier and merrier as time went on, till the evening, when, the fiddlers still scraping away and now producing sounds so queer that it was comforting to reflect that they had no smell to them. They would all retire to Old Whiting's beer-shop and finish up.

The vicar of East Blatchington, Robert Dennis, wrote in his diary for 1 May 1847:

Sweeps are dancing at my door with shovels and bells, fantastically dressed up in gilt paper caps, ribbons etc. A line of about 100 children with nosegays on the end of sticks have sallied forth from Rottingdean.

The Hastings Jack-in-the-Green custom has been well documented and well researched and revived by Keith Leech, Mad Jack's Morris and Hannah's Cat Morris, and is now part of a 'Green Man' festival over the early May bank holiday, though formerly on May Day itself. Local press records range from 1848 until 1913 and there is an archival photo from a collection published in 1913, which shows the Jack and several leaf clad figures outside the St Leonards' Subscription Gardens behind the Royal Victoria Hotel. The custom seems to have been brought in by the chimney-sweeping family of Lee from London in the 1840s, but to be in decline by the late 1870s. The abolition of climbing boys in 1864 affected the custom, as they had danced round the Jack and sometimes carried garlands.

The *Hastings News* of 5 May 1848 refers to 'The shovel and broom gentry' and 'the chevaliers of the soot-bag' on May Day, and quotes a poem:

Clowns, shovels, dust and noise
Jack in the Green, a sooty queen,
And half-a-dozen boys.

But by May 1883 *The Hastings and St Leonards Observer* is lamenting the end of the custom:

Have 'Jack' and his 'Green:' have 'my lord,' in his multi-coloured paper-patched coat, have 'my lady,' in her muslins, with her spoon gracefully extended for largesse; have the gentlemen of foolscap hats, and gay with many ribbons, and merry clown who was the most impudent and daring of varlets, always risking impaling himself upon an area of railings, when ladies at a parlour window were to be wheedled out of a few coins by his comical appeals to their purses; have the children-performers… —have all these … gone away?

The Morris Dance

The Morris Dance is recorded with the Jack in the Green at St Leonards in 1880, but Sussex does not seem to have the village Morris traditions of, say, the Cotswolds. But Morris dancers are mentioned from time to time at festive events, though whether they are local sides or hired from further afield it is difficult to say. The earliest Sussex account I have seen concerns a deposition to a Chichester magistrate in 1618 which refers to watching 'Morris dancers or maskers' at New Year. But Sussex has featured strongly in the second Morris revival (post 2nd World War), with Chanctonbury Morris leading the way from the 1950s and Broadwood and a fine ladies' side, Knots of May, who feature garland dances at the revival of the Good Friday skipping at Alciston at the Rose Cottage Inn, currently held at the Ram Inn, Firle.

Chanctonbury Morris, Good Friday Skipping 2014 Rose Cottage, Alciston. (*Geoff Doel*)

There are, however, several records of a Sussex 'Over the Sticks Dance', collected by Dorothy Marshall from Frank Albery of Borde Wood and Frank Dawtrey of Iping. *The Esperance Morris Dance Book,* volume 2 says of this: 'It is probable that this dance is the survival of one danced with flails, or frails as they are called locally… Mr Albery said he had heard tell of this dance being done over flails'.

One of the revival Mummers side, the Boxgrove Tipteerers, was photographed doing the dance at the end of their play by George Garland at Halnaker in 1936.

Oak Apple Day

Oak Apple Day (29 May) celebrated Charles II's birthday and his escape by hiding in an oak tree after the Battle of Boscobel. It was a public holiday until the early nineteenth century, with a celebratory church service and royalists wore oak. Fishing boat in the Brighton area (from where Charles had escaped to France by boat) were decorated by oak, as was the Kings Head pub in Brighton. In Sussex, 29 May was also known as 'Nettle Day' or 'Pinching Day' and if children didn't wear sprigs of oak, they would be called 'a dirty Puritan—and have the back of their legs beaten with nettles or being pinched. I remember as a child in Hove problems in finding oak in a built up area and using substitutes.

Whitsun

Whitsun was a moveable feast, now somewhat superseded by the late May bank holiday. The traditional Sussex repast on Whit Sunday was roast veal followed by gooseberry pudding. Whit Monday was formerly the meeting day for many of the benefit club society parades with elaborate banners. The benefit societies were an insurance against sickness and unemployment and were largely rendered obsolete by the National Health Service and sickness and unemployment benefit. Members made regular small monetary contributions as insurance against sickness, unemployment, and death. The club members met at regular intervals, usually in pubs, and in summer-time, as evidenced by numerous accounts in local nineteenth and early twentieth century and by many surviving photos, the annual club walks were enormous attractions. Club members put on their Sunday best, the men often wearing smocks and top hats, and carrying 6 foot peeled staves and paraded through the streets to music from the local band. A church service would follow and the day ended with a celebratory feast. The most famous, Harting Old Club, still flourishes. Tony Wales, in his *The West Sussex Village Book* mentions that in Albourne 'one little girl when asked by a school inspector to name the chief festivals of the church, replied 'Christmas, Easter and Albourne Club Day.'

At Barnes Green the club day was held on the third Monday in July and it was regarded as 'the biggest day of the year'. It was a school holiday and there was a procession led by a man in a white smock coat and members wearing rosettes and accompanied by a band. The procession went to Itchingfield Church for a special service, followed by mince pies and coffee at the rectory and later a lunch in a marquee at Mundham. A 'Cherry Fair' was held in a pub the night before

Club Day at Northiam early twentieth century. (*Tony Wales Collection*)

Village Club Day in Harting with Smocks, *c.* 1908.

and a fair on the village green on club day. Barnes Green Benefit Society was wound up in 1977 after 126 years and £6,000 was shared out amongst the thirty six remaining members.

Broadbridge Heath Club (near Horsham) was a fine affair in the nineteenth century, with members dressed in white smocks, fluffy beaver pot hats and coloured ribbon bows and carrying peeled willow staffs as they marched in procession to Horsham Church and back again to Broadbridge Heath for their feast and amusements.

Rogationtide: Beating the Bounds

A number of seasonal folk customs are perambulatory, the most obvious being the Beating of the Bounds, a ceremony often enacted at Rogationtide, which precedes Ascension Day, when the parish boundaries were walked and the younger generation symbolically beaten or bumped to aid their territorial memories. This is one of our earliest documented folk customs and the early Christian church seems to have been influenced in this by earlier cultures, such as the Roman celebration of Terminus, the god of boundaries, in whose honour the Romans processed through the fields at the festival of Ambarvalia.

Beating of the Bounds was regarded with suspicion by some early protestants and Puritans, but Elizabeth I re-affirmed permission for clergy, churchwardens and parishioners to process on Ascension Day to define parish boundaries and offer up prayers for fruitful crops. The ceremonies were organised through the church and the diocese of Chichester described their purpose in 1637 as for: 'knowing and distinguishing the bounds of the parishes, and for obtaining God's blessing upon the fruites of the ground.'

In 1777 the parish boundaries of Washington and Findon were beaten by the vicar, two gentlemen, a labourer and two youths. Beating of the bounds is recorded at Chailey in the seventeenth century and Tony Wales, in several of his excellent books on Sussex folklore draws attention to accounts of beating of the bounds at Burpham (1810) and Chiddingfold (1869). At Burpham the minister led the procession with the churchwardens and some members of the congregation, which stopped for prayers, the making of a cross on the ground and refreshments; 23 gallons of ale and quantities of bread and cheese and cake were provided. The Chiddingfold beating of the bounds involved a walk of 40 miles and took two days to complete; only three people took part! There is an account in the *Hampshire Telegraph* of 2 June 1828 of a beating of the bounds at Chichester:

> On Friday the Mayor of Chichester attended by some members of the Corporation, the sergeants and a posse of boys, according to ancient custom, perambulated the city bounds. The usual complement of sundry buckets of water, and two or three cold baths in the river Lavant, formed the principal features of the occasion, which ended with a sumptuous dinner at the Swan Inn.

Traditions survived until the nineteenth century at Littlehampton, to the early twentieth century at Barcombe and at Hastings until the 1920s; and I have seen a photo of an early twentieth century beating of the bounds at Lewes. A photo survives in the Bexhill Museum of the beating of the bounds at Bexhill in 1925, showing Mayor Sewell being bumped on boundary stone 34. A number of the boundary stones at Bexhill have recently been retrieved.

Beating the Bounds, Bexhill, 1935. Mayor Sewell bumped on boundary stone. (*Bexhill Museum*)

Beating the Bounds at Hastings, 1920.

Blessing the Sea at Hastings, 1920.

The beating of the bounds at Chailey was revived several times and has now become an annual event, with teams racing each other over the 24 miles, on foot and using bikes, horses and even canoes and wheelbarrows! The bounds are so long because they incorporate three villages—Chailey Green, South Common and North Common. Recent beating of the bounds include Crowborough, Southwick, Shoreham and Seaford. Tony Wales describes the most unusual beating of the bounds at The Flying Bull Inn Rake, where boys were put into the bread oven to remind them of the parish boundary which ran through the bar!

Another custom linked to Rogationtide is 'Blessing the Sea', which was revived at Hastings in Victorian times linked to the Fisherman's Church of St Nicholas. Shoreham and Lancing have followed suit.

Midsummer's Day

Sussex legends point to midsummer's eve as a time of supernatural happenings and for divination. There are legends of supernatural horses on Lancing Clump on midsummer's eve, of skeletons dancing round an old oak tree on Broadwater Green (North Worthing) until cock-crow and of those visiting Hollingbury Camp mysteriously finding themselves back at their starting-out-place in Hove.

As in Dorset, described by Thomas Hardy in his novel *The Woodlanders*, Sussex girls carried out divination practices to find the names or occupations of their future husbands, or the fidelity of their true loves and young men wore sprigs of the plant 'Live-long-love-long' (*sedum telephium*) to aid their courtship. St John's Wort (*hypericum perforatum*) was worn to keep witches away and Mugwort (*artemisia vulgaris*) was worn to prevent the spirits of the dead from capturing anyone falling asleep on this night.

Charlotte Latham mentions another tradition documented by Hardy in Dorset, the sowing of hempseed:

It is some time since I last heard of any young persons seeking to ascertain their matrimonial fate by sowing hemp-seed, but the old superstition still maintains its place in popular belief. The stout-hearted maiden must steal out alone to the church-yard, and sow a handful of hemp-seed, and pretend to harrow it with anything she can drag after her, saying

> *Hemp-seed, I sow thee,*
> *Hemp-seed, I sow thee;*
> *And he that is my true love*
> *Come after me and mow thee!*

And then she is to look over her left shoulder, and she will see a man mowing as he follows her. There are, however, only certain days in the year when the charm will take effect: one, if I remember right, is Midsummer, or St John's Eve, on which our ancestors used to practice so many superstitious observances; dancing around fires, crowned with garlands, and leaping over them… We no longer light our bonfires on the eve of good St John in Sussex, but some of the old superstitious feelings with respect to it still linger amongst us, and simple maidens have confessed in my hearing to their having, just before midnight, washed their sarks, and hung them out to dry before the kitchen fire, and waited to see who would come in and turn them. The kitchen door must be set wide open, or the charm will not work. In one case, I was informed, a very tall man in black came in and turned the sark, and then slowly walked away again.

Talking of her own experiences, Mrs Latham writes:

When we were children, we made Midsummer Men. These were two pieces of orpine, known to us as 'Live-long-love-long. These we pushed through two empty cotton reels and took them to bed with us. One reel was given the name of our particular boy friend and the other was ourself. In the morning we looked at the reels. If the plants had fallen towards each other, all was well. If they had fallen in one direction and the other in the opposite, then our love would not be true.

Little Edith's Treat

A curious custom takes place at my grandmother's village of Piddingoe, on the banks of the Ouse, near Newhaven, on 19 July, called 'Little Edith's Treat. When Edith Croft died in 1868 aged three months, her grandmother made an endowment of £100 to be spent on the baby's birthday. This is celebrated by a church service followed by children's races and tea.

Ebernoe Horn Fair

The wearing of horns was an ancient symbol of power and authority in many cultures, but by the sixteenth century in England it had become associated with cuckoldry and sexual loose conduct. The most famous horn fair was in October at Charlton in Kent and featured cross-dressing; it was banned by Act of Parliament, but has recently been revived. Sussex has a horn fair at Ebernoe held on St James's Day, 25 July, and a 'Horn Fair Song' collected by Vaughan Williams from Frederick Teal at Kingsfold, West Sussex, which is further evidence for the wearing of horns, though the song puzzlingly mentions spring.

> *As I was a-walking one morning in Spring,*
> *So soft blew the winds and the leaves growing green;*
> *I met a pretty damsel on a grey mare,*
> *As she was a -riding on to Horn Fair.*
>
> *I asked this pretty damsel for to let me ride.*
> *'O no, then: O no, my mammy would sigh:*
> *And besides my old daddy would bid me for sure*
> *And never let me ride on the grey mare any more.*
>
> *I can find by your talk you're for one game of play*
> *But you will not ride me nor my grey mare today:*

Ebernoe Horn Fair.

You will rumple my muslin and uncurl my hair
And I shouldn't be fit to be seen when I get to Horn Fair.

O, O my pretty damsel, how can you say so,
Since it is my intention Horn Fair to go?
We will join the best of company when we do get there
With horns on our heads as fine as our hair.

There were the finest of horns as ever you did behold,
There were the finest horns as were gilded with gold;
And ride merrily, merrily, Horn Fair we did go
Like jolly brisk couples, boys, and all in a row.

The song conveys the atmosphere and expectations of the horn fairs before their Victorian suppression. A fine rendering of this song by Sussex folk singer Bob Lewis can be found on the Veteran Tape *A Sweet Country Life* (VT120). Another possible link between ancient and modern is that the scandalous cross-dressing which occurred at the fair in earlier times is also a primitive symbol of fertility; an early saying is 'All's fair at Horn Fair'. The sexual elements and symbolism were toned down in the revival of 1864, where the focus switched to a cricket match between Ebernoe and a neighbouring village, during which a sheep was roasted, the horns being given to the batsman who scored the most runs.

Stray references in records in Kent and elsewhere suggest a number of horn fairs and a

Harvest North Bersted, *c.* 1908.

symbolic or legalistic use of the term; J. R. Chanter in a nineteenth century article on Devon customs mentions the nailing of horns to a church door as a claim to hold a cattle market as being described as 'horn fair'.

Harvest

The completion of the gathering in of the harvest had highly significant practical and symbolic meaning for farming communities. Wheat was the most important cereal crop grown in Sussex in the eighteenth and nineteenth centuries, with some oats, barley and rye. Today modern machinery ensures swift harvesting with a minimal workforce, but the harvesting of these cereals once involved whole communities. Lucy Baldwin and her brother, Arthur Ridsdale, describe the picturesque, if back-breaking harvesting of wheat in Rottingdean in the 1880s and the celebrations that followed:

> The harvest was cut with a reaping hook or sickle and then the swap hook. The straw was cut close to the ground. This sort of work was often given to men out of work or to tramps. They slept in hovels and barns whilst the harvest time lasted. After being cut by hand the bands were united together by two wisps of straw tied close to the ears by a particular knot and were then stacked in shocks or stooks. Occasionally a rabbit or two was found in the last part of the uncut corn and became 'perks' for those who caught them. After the cutting of the corn there came a small company of gleaners, children and adults, mostly women, to gather up the ears that were left. The village children's summer holidays always coincided with the harvest time, and it was a pretty sight, the elderly women wearing sun bonnets, they were worn then by all women over

Gleaners in the Fields of Southwick, 23 August 1892.

a certain age, as well as by some of the little girls. They used to do their gleaning in rows, the women first and the children behind, and the coloured sun bonnets were very attractive bobbing up and down.

When all the harvest was finished we had the harvest supper and harvest beer. The last load was carried in a large farm wagon with flags flying, many children and men sitting on top of the last load, while the carter led the horses. Healths were drunk in glorious beer, and boys and men sang in chorus the following refrain:

> *We plough, we sow, we reap, we mow,*
> *We've carried our last load and ain't other (over) throwed!*
> *Hip, hip, hurrah etc.*

They pulled up at each public house and each private residence in turn as they went the round of the village.

The large barn at Court Farm, near the church, faced north and had large double folding doors; the other doors looked into the farmyard. In the barn wheat and oats were stored. There one heard the flail in constant use and also the old winnowing machine which was turned by hand and made much dust. The floor was made of ground ash, which soon became polished and very hard.

It was traditional to lave a little in the fields for the poorer members of the community to harvest as gleaners. A lady of 92 remembered the harvest celebrations at Goring in 1840-52 in an article in the *Sussex County Magazine* in 1927:

Felpham Harvest Home, 1869.

After harvesting they all stood in a ring in the stack-yard and shouted:

> *We've ploughed, we've sowed, we've reaped, we've mowed,*
> *We've carried our last harvest load!*
> *Hip, hip, hip, hooray!*
> *Send out the maids with ribands flying*
> *God mistress with the steddle-cup,*
> *For we with drouth comes near a-dying,*
> *And we has set our last sheaf up.*
> *Hip, hip, hip, hooray.*

A harvest supper was usually provided on a Saturday by the farmer(s). Tony Wales describes the harvest home of 1863 at West Hoathly:

> The day began at 8 a.m. with the church bells ringing. The main street was decorated with flags and greenery, and at 1.30 p.m. a service was held in the church. This was followed by a procession led by the village band; farmers had provided wagons and there were such things in the parade as a huge loaf of bread carried on a wooden tray. The landowners had contributed two shillings each to contribute to the feast, which was held in a marquee in Cross Field. The meal included quantities of beef, potatoes, suet pudding, plum cake, and gingerbread. The wives and children had a separate tent, in which they had a lighter meal of tea and cakes. Afterwards, those who were in a fit state were invited to take part in sports, with various prizes.

Although hop-picking in associated strongly with neighbouring Kent, there were a lot of hops grown in East Sussex, and numerous former oast houses with conical roves are scattered across the landscape. Hops were usually ready for harvesting in late August and early September and many migrant hop pickers descended on the Sussex farms for a few weeks for holidays with pay. Travelling communities and Londoners came in large quantities—the men sometimes at weekends from other employments, and lots of women and children were involved. Up until the late 1950s, fields full of 6-metre poles carrying networks of strong wire which supported the growing hops, men on stilts walking up and down the rows, and the hop-pickers' huts, often of corregated iron, were a common sight.

The hop pole puller was an important job often allocated to a regular farm-hand. As he had close links with the pickers, as he offered the bines to them when uprooting the poles, there were often rituals involving puller and picker. Thomas Turner in his diary for 1756 mentions for 20 September that 'In the even, Mr Porter's hoppers bought their pole puller's nickcloth' and for 23 September 'Halland hop-pickers bought their pole-puller's nickcloth; and, poor wretches, many of them insensible'.

At the end of the hop harvest were celebrations. Many farms had tea parties for the hoppers' children, followed by a hopping supper for the adult workers in the evening, often in the oast houses. On some farms there was an election of a King and Queen of the Hops—in earlier times they were thrown into the bins—and drinking, music and dancing. The pickers wore hats decorated with dog daisies, convolvulus, tulip, cornflowers and, of course, hops.

9

The Shepherds of the Downs

R. W. Blencowe's fascinating article 'South-Down Shepherds and Their Songs at the Sheepshearing' (1849) looks back to the eighteenth century when:

> Here and there only… along its southern slopes, or in the bottom of its valleys, was the land under tillage; over all the rest were spread vast flocks of sheep, which, with their attendant shepherds, ranged over a thousand breezy hills.
>
> Few people, probably, are aware of the immense number of sheep which, under the twofold impulse of foreign demand and that given to it by the great woollen manufacture at home were reared in England at an early period of our history.

The Southdown breed of sheep, developed in the eighteenth century by John Ellman, was enormously successful. John was born in Hartfield in 1753 and moved with his parents to Place Farm in Glynde in 1761 and inherited the tenancy of this in 1780. By breeding he changed the Southdown breed from a tall and lean sheep into a broader and lower sheep, which retained its fine quality fleece, but vastly improved the mutton yield and quality. A later member of the family (also called John) contributed an article on Southdown sheep to Thomas Horsfield's book on Sussex in 1835:

> Of their breed of sheep this county may be truly proud. To have spread, as Southdown sheep have done, from this part of the kingdom to the remotest corner of Great Britain and Ireland, is a regular proof of what may be done by intelligence … When we reflect that forty years have scarcely elapsed since the South-down sheep were not known, except in this county and part of Kent and Surrey, and that now, go to what part of England you may, you meet with them on poor land, where they have supplanted the native sheep of the district, a South-down farmer may really be proud of his tithe. In Hampshire, Wiltshire, Dorsetshire, Berkshire, Norfolk, all once famous for the sheep which beat those names, we scarcely find any but South-Down … (thanks to) the care and attention of the late Mr. Ellman in improving the breed.

Blencowe stresses the usual solitude of the shepherd's life on the South Downs, except in the month of June when the sheepshearing was a social time:

Above: Steve Barrow, Shepherd at Rottingdean.

Left: John Ellman, improver of Southdown Sheep breed. (*James Lonsdale, Lewes Castle & Museum*)

when they met together in considerable numbers to shear the various flocks. Their work was hard; but there was much that was enjoyable in it, for it was a season of social merriment, which contrasted strongly with the usual solitary tenor of their lives.

The shearing used to be performed by companies, consisting generally of above thirty men, and most of them formerly were shepherds. Each company received its distinctive name from some place within the sphere of its labours. One was called, for instance, the Brookside, another the Portslade Company; each of them had a captain and lieutenant placed over it, and these men, selected by the party for their trustworthy character, their superior intelligence, and their skill in the shearing art, exhibited a pleasant specimen of a good elective government. Nor were the outward symbols of authority wanting, for the captain was distinguished by his gold-laced, and the lieutenant by his silver-laced hat …

As soon as the company was formed, all the men repaired to the cottage of the captain, where a feast, which was called the 'White ram', was provided for them, and on this occasion the whole plan of the campaign was discussed and arranged.

They generally got to their place of shearing about seven, and having breakfasted, began their work. Once in the forenoon and twice in the afternoon, their custom was 'to light up,' as they termed it; they ceased to work for a few minutes, drank their beer, sharpened their shears, and set to work again: their dinner-hour was one, but this was not the great meal of the day, their supper being the time of real enjoyment, and when this was over, they would remain for several hours in the house, smoking their pipes, and singing their sheepshearing songs, in which they were joined by the servants of the farm, and sometimes the master and mistress of the house would favour them with their presence. The following was a favourite song:

> *Come, all my jolly boys, and we'll together go*
> *Abroad with our masters, to shear the lamb and ewe;*
> *All in the merry month of June, of all times in the year,*
> *It always comes in season the ewes and lambs to shear;*
> *And there we must work hard, boys, until our backs do ache,*
> *And our master he will bring us beer whenever we do lack.*
>
> *Our master he comes round to see our work is doing well,*
> *And he cries, 'Shear them close, men, for there is but little wool.'*
> *'O yes, good master,' we reply, 'we'll do well as we can.'*
> *When our captain calls, 'Shear close, boys!' to each and every man;*
> *And at some places still we have this story all day long,*
> *'Close them boys! And shear them well!' and this is all their song.*
>
> *And then our noble captain doth unto our master say,*
> *'Come, let us have one bucket of your good ale, I pray.'*
> *He turns unto our captain, and makes him this reply:*
> *'You shall have the best of beer, I promise presently.'*
> *Then out with the bucket pretty Betsy she doth come,*
> *And master says, 'Maid, mind and see that every man has some.'*

This is some of our pastime while we the sheep do shear,
And though we are such merry boys, we work hard, I declare;
And when 'tis night, and we have done, our master is more free,
And stores us well with good strong beer, and pipes and tobaccee.
So we do sit and drink, we smoke, and sing and roar,
Till we become more merry far than e'er we were before.

When all our work is done, and all our sheep are shorn,
Then home to our captain, to drink the ale that's strong.
'Tis a barrel, then, of hum cap, which we call the black ram;
And we do sit and swagger, and swear that we are men;
But yet before 'tis night, I'll stand you half a crown,
That if you ha'n't a special care, the ram will knock you down.

When the supper was finished, and the profits shared, they all shook hands and parted, bidding each other good-bye till another year.

The social mirth has of late years very much abated, for since it has ceased to be the custom to shear the lambs as well as the ewes, the number of men in each company has much lessened, and now the shearers frequently bring their own provisions with them, and board themselves, perhaps never entering the master's house at all.

R. W. Blencowe's source for this information was a former shepherd, John Dudeney of Lewes, born in 1782 the son and grandson of shepherds. He mentioned that his mother looked after the flock whilst his father went sheep-shearing. At sixteen he was under-shepherd at West Blatchington and in 1799 he was appointed under-shepherd at Kingston near Lewes looking

Sheep at Falmer Dew Pond, 1920s.

after a flock of 1400 'winter stock' for £6 a year wages, supplemented by selling wheat-ears and moles. The head shepherd at Kingston:

> had the keeping of twenty sheep as part of his wages; and I have heard old shepherds affirm, that in the generation before them, some of the shepherds had nearly all, or quite all, their wages in this way, and it seems to have been of very ancient practice.

He then became head shepherd at Westside Farm:

> extending from Rottingdean to Black Rock, in Brighton parish; it was a long, narrow slip of ground, not averaging more than half a mile in width. My flock required very close attention, as they had to feed so much between the pieces of corn, and there were no fences to keep them off. In such situations a good dog is a most valuable help to a shepherd, and I was fortunate in having a very excellent one.

An account survives in *Sussex Notes and Queries* of resolutions adopted at a meeting of the 'Company of Sheep Shearers' at the Swan Inn, Falmer on Wednesday 21 May 1828:

> 1st—That the Men must be at the place they are going to work at 7 o'clock in the morning, they shall then immediately go to breakfast and be in the Barn ready to go to work at 8. To be allowed cold meat, or meat pies for their breakfast and one quart of Ale each man.
>
> 2nd—That they shall light up twice in the forenoon and be allowed each time one pint of Ale each man.
>
> 3rd—That they have at dinner boiled Meat, Meat Puddings, or Pies, what small beer they like and half a pint of Strong Beer each Man after Dinner.
>
> 4th—That they be allowed to light up twice in the afternoon, that they have a Pint of mixed beer half Ale and half strong the first time, and at the other, a Pint of Ale each Man.
>
> 5th—That they be allowed cold Meat and Bread and Cheese for Supper, one Quart of Ale each Man, with One Pint of Strong Beer a Man after Supper. That they are to be allowed one hour and a half for Supper and to drink their Beer and that no smoking or singing be allowed.
>
> 6th—That they have 10*d* per score for Ewes, Lambs and Tags when the whole are shorn, and 18*d* per score for Ewes and Tags, 14*d* per score for Lambs, when only a part are shorn, to have 20*d* per score for Shearing a Wether Flock, and in case any employer wishes to limit the number of his sheep to be shorn in one day to a less number than 40 per Man, the Company to be paid for that limited number the same as if 40 were shorn. To have 1*s* per hundred for winding, 3*d* a 100 for Black Lamb and 2*s* 6*d* per day extra for the captain and 1*s* for the Tar Boy.
>
> ...7th—That in case of wet weather, the Men to have a Breakfast as usual, with a Quart of Ale, and wait till their employer pleases to see if there is any probability of Shearing and Sheep that day.

Clearly sheep-shearing was thirsty work! The reference to no singing be allowed' in rule 5 is rather a puzzle, and must just be a specific context as we hear of many songs being sung, some specifically about sheep-shearing, as for example 'The Rosebud in June' cited by R. W. Blencowe:

> *Here the rose buds in June, and the violets are blowing,*
> *The small birds they warble from every green bough;*
> *Here's the pink and the lily,*

And the daffydowndilly,
To adorn and perfume the sweet meadows in June.
'Tis all before the plough the fat oxen go slow;
But the lads and the lasses to the sheepshearing go.

Sheep Washing

Before the shearing the sheep were washed at various pools or in rivers, such as the Arun as pools and running water were scarce on the Downs. The spring of clear water rising at Fulking was highly suitable and many other downland villages sent their sheep there to be washed at the end of May, or early June before shearing. A landlady of the picturesque inn The Shepherd and Dog at Fulking noted down in 1851 her memories of sheep washing at the roadside spring nearby, which now has a religious text by it:

> Thousands of sheep were brought to be washed by the men in the spring water. They paid half-a-crown a hundred for washing. The last item on each account was 'so much for the Black Ram', the Black Ram being the dinner which was always given by the farmers to the men at the end of the washing.

A dam was made to hold the stream, whilst the sheep were kept in readiness in a pen. The washing was carried out by two or three men who stood in the cold water for several hours. They met at the pub to plan their programme in what was called 'White Ram Night'. At the end of shearing a celebratory dinner was held at The Shepherd and Dog with singing. Arrangements were made for the following year, the gathering being called 'Black Ram Night'.

Sheep bells

Arthur Beckett in *The Wonderful Weald* says:

> Concerning sheep-bells you should note that if you hear them close at hand they sound harsh and untuneful, but, given a little distance, the harshness vanishes, the tunes are softened and melodious. So clearly do some of the shepherds hear them that they will tell you the name of the owner of a flock without seeing it, merely from the sound of its bells.

Sheep Fairs

Findon sheep fair was established on 14 September 1790, with permission from the lord of the manor, William Richardson. Horsfield comments in 1835 that it:

> Is now of importance, and attended by the principal graziers in Sussex. About one thousand ewes and two thousand lambs are penned. There is generally a good show of horned cattle, horses, pigs etc.

A lamb fair was established at Findon on 14 July.

Sheep Washing in Sussex, 1889. (*James Aumonier*)

A Flock of Sheep by Jill. (*Barclay Wills*)

Findon Sheep Fair.

Shepherds Huts

Mark Lower in 1854 commented on the disappearance of shepherds' huts:

> You very seldom see a shepherd's hut on our hills in these times, but formerly every shepherd had one. Sometimes it was a sort of cave dug in the side of a bank or link, and had large stones inside. It was commonly lined with heath or straw. The part above ground was covered with sods of turf or heath or straw. The part above ground was covered with sods of turf or heath or straw or boughs of hawth. In rough, shruckish weather the shepherd used to turn into his hut and lie by the hour together, only looking out once in a while to see that the sheep didn't stray too far. Here he was safe and dry, however the storm might blow over-head, and he could sit and amuse himself as he liked best.

Nelson Coppard and Making a Lamb 'Take'

Barclay Wills, a Londoner by birth, developed a passionate love of the Downs and moved to Sussex, finally living in Worthing. He walked incessantly over the Downs and became personally known to many of the shepherds and wrote three books about their way of life. A favourite shepherd of his was Nelson Coppard, who over the years worked at Horton near Beeding, Patcham, Saddlescombe, Trueleigh, Iford, Falmer and Clayton. He watched Mr Coppard skin a dead lamb and cover a lamb who had lost its mother with it. Then the mother of the dead lamb, full of milk, was induced to suckle the substitute. Barclay Wills wrote:

> There is always something of interest or something quaint to note down after a visit to Nelson … He was the first shepherd I ever met. From him I had my first instruction on sheep-bells, crooks and the details of a shepherd's life.

Nelson earned *2s 6d* a week until he became a fully fledged shepherd, when he earned 12 shillings a week plus 1s 6d for his dog. His usual dress was 'good corduroy suits and gaiters, with a hard felt bowler hat'; his father had worn a blue smock.

Sheep Crooks

Sheep crooks from Pyecombe Forge were distinctive and famous. Mr Berry was the blacksmith there from about 1820 until 1855, and he invented he famous Pyecombe style of crook. He was succeeded for about 60 years, by George Mitchell. The two Sussex shepherds depicted on the manger scene in the Bloomsbury Group Berwick murals, both have Pyecombe crooks. There is also a traditional Sussex 'trug' or basket in the mural.

Shepherds' Wedding Customs

Hone's *Everyday Book* for 1827 reports:

Lifting is a custom practiced with hurdles among shepherds, in the South Downs at their marriages. The bride and bridegroom are carried round a flock of sheep; a fleece is put for their seat, and may-horns made of the rind of the sycamore tree, are played by boys and girls.

Shepherds' Burial Customs

Barclay Wills in his book *Shepherds of Sussex* says:

A custom which was once always practiced in Downland, and is still in some villages, is the placing of a lock of sheep's wool on the breast of a shepherd at his burial, so that—Downlanders say—he may be able, on Resurrection Day, to hold it up as proof of the calling which kept him up on the hills and far away from the church on Sundays.

Shepherds were allowed to take their dogs to church until 1800

Proverbial Sayings

According to Charlotte Latham, 'we speak figuratively of the one black sheep that is the cause of sorrow in a family; but in reality, it is regarded by the Sussex shepherd as an omen of good luck to his flock'.

10

Fisher Folk and Dippers

Fisher Folk at Brighton

Although Brighton was not important enough in the middle ages to be a Cinque port and did not have a harbour, a significant fishing economy, particularly in mackerel and herring developed there and considerable detail is known, thanks partly to its links with the local St Bartholomew's Priory. The Domesday male population of Brighthelmstone was only 90 and the Brighthelmstone annual payment was 4,000 herrings or mackerel, compared with 38,500 for Southease and 16,000 for Iford, both in the Ouse valley.

Originally the Brighton fishermen paid tithes in fish to St Bartholomew's Priory and the parish church. It was in the Elizabethan period that fishing became really significant at Brighton, with records of 400 mariners, 10,000 nets and 102 landsmen. Below the cliff was a long street of little tenements, stretching from the Steyne for more than a quarter of a mile towards Hove. The Sackvilles, as lords of the manor, displaced the priory, but the protestant church still received tithes. Because of these changes and the expansion of the fishing industry, the Brighton fishermen demanded rights and a commission was set up and a settlement was drawn up in 1580 enshrined in 'The Book of all the Auncient Customs', which refers to 80 fishing boats.

The 'Brighton Custumal' describes a system of 'fares' and 'shares' for the mackerel season (mid-April–mid-June) and for other fishing; the catch or its value was divided between the master of the ship, men, vicar and churchwardens and defence of the town from the French. These procedures were more of less still in place when Horsfield wrote in 1835:

At the present time (from the beginning of the season till Midsummer Day, but not at any other time of the year) the fishermen pay to the lord six mackerels for each boat, every time they return from mackerel fishing, and have taken more than a hundred fish. The fish thus paid to the manor is now called 'Reve', or more properly reves, which signifies rents or tythes, from the Saxon verb 'refian', 'to exact'.

The majority of the population were engaged in maritime occupations, and principally as fishermen. Their labours were not confined to the sea washing their immediate coast, but indeed, either by the scarcity of fish on their own shores, or by the more profitable speculation of distant

Brighton Fishermen. (*Juvenile Varieties early 19th century*)

enterprise, they ventured from home, and found on the coast of Scarborough, cod-fish sufficient to reward their toil, or at the bank of Great Yarmouth an abundance of herrings to remunerate them for absence from their families during two or three months in every year. The boats which they used in these distant fisheries were from 15 to 40 tons burden, with an average of about 12 men in each; the produce was divided into shares, of which the vicar, the town, and the master, always claimed one, i.e. a quarter share to the churchwardens of Brighthelmstone, for the time being, half a share to the vicar, and the other quarter to the master of the boat.

The Brighton traditional fishing boats were called Hog boats, and were short and bulky and from 8 to 12 tons. The mainmast was placed forward of midships, supported by two shrouds and a stay, which extended to an out-rigger or prow, projecting from the stern. On ordinary occasions the hog-boat carried a sprit mainsail, a very large foresail, and a spritmizen; sometimes a jib was added in fine weather, but very rarely a topsail. Because of its flat bottom, the hog-boat used a leeboard, to keep it as near the wind as possible. It sailed with ballast trimmed to windward to preserve keel and was launched over troughs, being checked in its descent over the beach by a 'shock-anchor', and, when nearly afloat, was hauled clear of the surf by means of a rope extending from a crank at the foot of the mainmast to an anchor some distance at sea, which was left for the purpose on the sands at low-water.

Houses to the south of Brighton under the cliff were destroyed by storms and eroded by the sea, but by 1750 Brighton had about 400 dwellings and a population of about 2,000. Half the population relied on marine activity, the largest group being fishermen. By 1761 there were 57 fishing boats and 300 working fishermen, often styled 'mariners', for example on the wedding certificate of one of my ancestors in the mid-nineteenth century. The distinction between 'fisherman' and 'mariner' at Brighton seems imprecise, but the latter is

The Fishmarket Brighton, early 1900s.

more often used in the past for skilled practitioners on ship or owners of maritime businesses ashore. For example, the 'mariners' funded the building of a Block House near to the Black Lion to protect the town from further French raids.

In the 1770s Brighton's fishing community was described in both national and local guides as 'a sober, industrious body of people, employed throughout the greatest part of the year in a succession of labour'. On the Steine fishermen could be seen maintaining their boats, women, 'busy in preparing the nets, to be made use by their husbands in the fishery', shipwrights making 'small barks for the merchants of London and other ports.'

About 1800 Thomas Pennant reported that in the spring nets 'thirty-six to fifty yards long and deep' are 'spread upon the Steine; a privilege, of time immemorial, granted to the fishermen. The boats are drawn on shore at the latter end of the winter, and placed in ranges on the lower part of the Steine.' Pennant says that the—'boats were from ten to fifteen tuns burthen, remarkably stout built and having a crew of three or four men with one boy. For mackerel fishing there were about 45 boats and 25 for trawling'.

With the coming of the Prince of Wales and the building of the Royal Pavilion, Brighton began to view the fishery as a nuisance which obstructed visitors. One visitor noted in 1799:

Fishing-nets are daily spread from one end of the Stayne to the other, so that company, while walking, are frequently tripped up by entangling their feet; and if any of the barbarians to whom the nets belong should be standing by, you are sure to be reprobated and insulted for what you can not avoid.

The fishermen began to be referred to as 'Brighton's aborigines' and the town commissioners were systematically stripping away the 'ancient rites' enjoyed by the fishing community since 'time out of mind'. In the early nineteenth century there were 80 fishing boats in a population of well over 7,000 and the fishermen seen as 'a race apart', living in tenements (since destroyed by the sea) stretching from the Steyne to Hove. Harrison Ainsworth, in his novel *Ovingdean Grange*, says:

> These tenements were exclusively inhabited by fishermen and boatmen, a bold and hardy, though somewhat troublesome race, who claimed for themselves certain privileges and immunities and were uncommon and indeed, pugnacious, in the maintenance of their supposed rights.

By 1830 the population had jumped to 40,000, which included 300 fishermen. The census of 1841 showed 224 fishermen and that of 1851 244 fishermen. The railway brought North Sea fish cheaper than the local catch. Also, as land prices soared with new building, many fishing families were forced to move from their small houses with 'plots or gardens for the production of hemp'.

The decline of the fishing industry is discussed by Horsfield in 1835:

> The few fish that are caught here are exposed for sale immediately, from the boats on the beach … They are sold in small quantities to the fish-women; the seller names a price, and reduces the sum asked until he meets with a purchase. After this mock- auction is over, the fish is sold retail to private individuals.

Some fish wives came from as far inland as Lewes, walking 8 miles each way to collect and sell their fish and were called 'Juggs'; there is a surviving footpath, the Juggs Way from Lewes to Brighton.

Mr Michel, writing in Dr Relham's *Brighthelmstone* in about 1830, also charts the decline of the past 30 years:

> It is a melancholy reflection to compare the present state of the fishery with its prosperity in 1579, or in more modern periods. Within the recollection of this editor, there were sixty boats employed in catching mackerel; and in a prosperous season, that species of fish has produced in Billingsgate market a sum of £10,000, with which the town was enriched. In the autumn, twenty of these boats were fitted out for the herring voyage; and one boat has been known to land during the season from twenty to thirty lasts of herrings, each last containing 10,000 fish… In the mackerel season 1829, as in that preceding, twenty boats only were employed, and very few fitted out for the herring voyage.

Charles Fleet describes the beach fishing industry in the mid-nineteenth century by which time the fishermen were only 3 per cent of the adult male working population, though it still had the largest fishing fleet in the region with over 130 boats. At this time 245 fishermen lived in Brighton, 192 in Hastings, 51 in Eastbourne and 41 in Worthing. The fleet expanded to 150 boats by the 1860s, supported by the Town Council by the creation of a purpose built fishing quarter.

Mackerel Fishing and Bending-In at Brighton

Mackerel fishing was very important in Brighton and the season started on 1 May, roughly when the shoals of mackerel, which come up-channel from Cornwall, start to arrive in the area. Brighton fishermen often garlanded their boats on May Day and they gave children a ritual meal called 'bending in, described by Frederick Sawyer:

There still exists in Brighton a curious custom called 'Bending-in', consisting of a meal of bread and cheese, or bread and treacle, given by the fishermen prior to commencing mackerel fishing, to the children who may be on the beach. The word 'bending-in' is probably corrupted from 'benediction', as the Vicar of Brighton was entitled to a share in the profits of the fishing boats, the benediction of the Church was doubtless prudently and far-sightedly bestowed upon the fishermen before commencing their labours, possibly also the communion was administered to them in addition, and so originated the present meal of bread and cheese. Amusement in the shape of 'Punch and Judy' is sometimes provided for the children, and the children, after eating, wish good luck to the owners of the fishing-boats. When casting over the nets to commence mackerel and herring fishing, each night the Brighton fishermen stand round with their hats off, no swearing being allowed, and the master stands aft. They then repeat the following quaint hymn or prayer:

> *There they goes, then; God Almighty*
> *Send us a blessing, it is to be hoped*

As each 'barrel' (which is attached to every ten nets out of the 'fleet', or 120 nets) is cast overboard, they say:

Brighton Fishermen landing a catch of mackerel, early 1900s.

Watch barrel, watch! Mackerel for to catch.
White may they be, lie blossom on a tree.
God send thousands, one, two, and three.
Some by their heads, some by their tails.
God sends thousands, and never fails.

When the last net is overboard the master says: 'Seas all!' and then lowers the foremast and lays to the wind.

The Hastings Fishermen

The most picturesque part of Hastings is the Old Town which is the fishermen's quarter. The fishing industry has undergone many changes since the first net-lofts were set up on the beach in the sixteenth century but a even today a crowd of distinctive black-tarred two and three storied lofts still house some of the fishermen's big nets and other gear on the beach while the local fishing boats are still hauled up on the shingles as there is no natural harbour. The nearby Fishermen's Museum built in 1854 was originally the Fishermen's Chapel. Sandra Collins of the Museum gives this account of local Christmas and New Year customs:

The Winkle Club of Hastings 'set up to help the poor fishermen and their families' used their funds to organise an annual party for the children of fishermen which was given on New Year's Day or as near to that festival as possible. One of the really exciting moments was when Father Christmas would arrive on the beach by fishing boat. The fishermen used to tie a Christmas tree

Hastings Fishermen.

to the foremast of their boats ... Around 1940 a Mrs Terrell would arrange magic lantern shows for the children in the Wesleyan Chapel in the Bourney, Hastings. The children would save a penny a week for 12 weeks and receive a Christmas stocking of sweets and fruit and maybe a small toy.

The sea is blessed annually at Hastings. On the Wednesday before Ascension Day, the rectors of All Saints and St Clements churches lead an evening procession to hold a service on the lifeboat, with hymns including 'Abide With Me' and 'Eternal Father Strong to Save', prayers and a formal blessing. Lancing has started the practice.

Wrecking

Legendary accounts of coastal communities deliberately wrecking vessels in order to access the cargoes of ships have not been borne out by the facts. The contrary was often the case, with great efforts being made to save life. However, once ships were wrecked, coastal communities have always regarded items being washed up on the shore as gifts to them from the sea and is has been difficult for the owners of wrecked cargoes to reclaim them. The legal situation has changed frequently, from Anglo-Saxon law to the present day, but up until the nineteenth century the lord of the manor where the goods were washed up, had a claim on them. Horsfield describes the complex legal situation at Brighton:

> All wrecks or goods washed by the sea on this manor, belong to the lords, but if any find them before the lord's servants, a moiety of the things so found belong to the finder. They are accordingly valued by the homage of the manor, at the next court baron held there.

Sussex was renowned for communities seizing wrecked goods. And it must be admitted that evidence suggests that at times Sussex coastal communities longed for wrecks and seemed indifferent to the suffering these caused. In the epilogue to his play *The Mourning Bride* (1697) William Congreve compares drama critics to the 'Sussex men that dwell upon the shore', who:

> *Look out when storms arise, and billows roar,*
> *Devoutly praying, with uplifted hands,*
> *That some well-laden ship may strike the sands;*
> *To whose rich cargo they may make pretence,*
> *And fatten on the spoils of Providence.*

A pamphlet was published by an eye-witness concerning the stranding of seven ships in Seaford Bay in 1809:

> Horror rivets my heart as I write it, among the humane and feeling many, there were still those monsters of rapine to be found, who, regardless of the fates of the tempest-beaten seamen, untouched by the agonized shrieks of the exhausted and the dying, were intent on plunder only; nor could the ghastly corps that, at intervals, the tide cast between them and the objects they were grasping at, for an instant suspend their horrible and infamous purpose.

Another 'wrecking' incident at Seaford in 1836 witnessed hundred of wreckers looting the cargoes.

Dippers

Just as the fishing declined at Brighton, medical endorsement of the efficacy of sea air and sea bathing created a new economic basis for prosperity at Brighton and other Sussex ports, which developed into coastal resorts. Brighton was patronized by royalty, notably the Prince Regent. This gave a seasonal boost to local employment through boat trips, the hiring of bathing machines and the employment of local men and women, often fishermen and fish wives, as 'dippers'. The novel *The Expedition of Humphry Clinker* by Tobias Smollett (1771) describes a bathing machine:

> Imagine to yourself a small, snug, wooden chamber, fixed upon a wheel-carriage, having a door at each end, and on each side a little window above, a bench below. The bather, ascending into this apartment by wooden steps, shuts himself in, and begins to undress, while the attendant yokes a horse to the end next the sea, and draws the carriage forwards, till the surface of the water is on a level with the floor of the dressing-room, then he moves and fixes the horse to the other end.—The person within being stripped, opens the door to the sea-ward, where he finds the guide ready, and plunges headlong into the water.—After having bathed, he re-ascends into the apartment, by the steps which had been shifted for that purpose, and puts on his clothes at his leisure, while the carriage is drawn back again upon the dry land; so that he has nothing further to do, but to open the door, and come down as he went up.—Should he be so weak or ill as to require a servant to put off and on his clothes, there is room enough in the apartment for half a dozen people.

The majority of sea bathers in the late eighteenth and early nineteenth century seem to have been female, as were many of the 'dippers', strong attendants who would help bathers in and out of the sea, sometimes tying a rope around the waist of non-swimmers and they would keep an eye on the bathers in case they got into difficulty. At Brighton, some of the 'dippers' became celebrities, in particularly Martha Gunn, one of the dippers of the Prince Regent. *The Morning Herald* in August 1806, quoted by Clifford Musgrave in his *Life of Brighton*, paints the scene:

> The Beach this morning was thronged with ladies, all anxious to make interest for a dip. The machines, of course, were in very great request, though none could be run into the ocean in consequence of the heavy swell, but remained stationary at the water's edge, from which Martha Gunn and her robust female assistants took their fair charges, closely enveloped in their partly coloured dresses, and gently held them to the breakers, which not quite so gently passed over them.

'Smoaker' Miles was another of the prince's dippers and he and Martha Gunn are celebrated in contemporary verse:

Above left: The Bather (Martha Gunn) (*Juvenile Varieties, early 19th century*)

Above right: Martha Gunn.

There's plenty of dippers and jokers,
And salt-water ripe for your fun,
The King of 'em all is Old Smoaker,
The Queen of 'em all Old Martha Gunn.

To Brighton came he
Came George the Third's Son.
To be bathed in the sea,
By famed Martha Gunn.

An anecdote recounts a conversation between the Prince and Smoaker:

'I shall bathe this morning, Smoaker.'
'No, no, Your Royal Highness, it's too dangerous.'
'But I will,'
'come, come, this won't do… I'll be damned if you shall bathe. What do you think your royal father would think of me if you were drowned? He would say, 'this is all owing to you, Smoaker. If you had taken proper care of him, poor George would still be alive.'

11

Smuggling

Customs duties date from Saxon times, when King Ethelred II imposed an import duty on boatloads of foreign wine arriving at Billingsgate. Thereafter it became a 'custom' for foreign vintners to give up some portion of their cargoes in return for permission to trade. Such tolls applied only to certain ports. In 1275, Edward I introduced a custom on wool exports. To collect duties a permanent customs staff was established. The first major smuggling was therefore export smuggling and smugglers were known along the south coast as 'owlers' owing to their night time activity, who smuggled raw wool across the Channel to avoid the severe restrictions protecting the English weaving industry. The supervisor of customs in Kent and Sussex complained in 1697 that most of the fleece shorn from the 160,000 sheep on Romney Marsh would be sent "hot into France". Import smuggling became significant in the eighteenth century, with the considerable import duties levied on luxury items such as brandy, rum, tobacco, tea, silks and muslins; so high were these duties, that smugglers could sell goods for as little as a quarter of their import price and still make a good profit.

The Cinque Ports

Seaford, Pevensey, Hastings, Winchelsea and Rye were linked with the Federation of Cinque Ports, with a duty to provide shipping in times of war and benefits which often included duty free imports. Each town enjoyed the privileges and had to discharge the obligations, which their respective charters required. There was a genuine grievance in the Cinque Ports when these arrangements, including duty free access, were abolished. As a consequence, the Cinque ports fell on hard times and many of the inhabitants took up smuggling; Hastings was one of the primary Cinque Ports and Winchelsea and Rye, the two 'ancient towns' had joined with the five to form The Cinque Ports Federation. Winchelsea's famous wine trade declined, partly due to import duties and the loss of Cinque Ports privileges and it turned to smuggling instead. Adam Smith, an advocate of free trade, defined a smuggler as:

A person who, though no doubt highly blamable for violating the laws of his country, is frequently incapable of violating those of natural justice and who would have been in every respect an excellent citizen had not the laws of his country made that a crime which Nature never meant to be so.

Smuggling assisted whole communities within reach of the coast and was often discreetly supported by gentry and clergy and many of the local legends about smuggling show an amused tolerance at the outwitting of authority. Churches were often used for storing tubs—there is a legend of St Andrews, Hove church being so used in my family traditions and the story is also told in Victor Cook's *The Story of Sussex*:

> The parishes of Hove and Preston were, in the days before Hove grew up, served by one parson, the services being taken at each Parish Church on alternate Sundays. The story goes that one Hove Sunday the vicar in full canonicals went to the church to do his office. To his surprise, the bell was not ringing, and on his enquiring the reason of the sexton, that artist calmly informed him that he had made a mistake, and that it was 'Preston Sunday.' The vicar stuck to it that he was right, and the sexton as stoutly maintained that he was wrong. The vicar would not admit that he was in error, and ordered the bell to be rung for service. 'It's no use, sir,' said the sexton at last. 'You can't preach today.' 'Why not?' demanded the angry parson. 'Because the church is full of tubs, and the pulpit's full of tea.'

Farmers lent horses and carts, labourers carried tubs at night to earn extra money, juries were reluctant to convict smugglers and magistrates often gave lenient sentences such as fines for those who were convicted.

Evidence in the excise returns of the late eighteenth century suggests that a quarter of British smuggling vessels operated from Kent and Sussex and that over half the gin smuggled into Britain and a third of the tea was smuggled into Kent and Sussex, counties near both to the Continent and to London. Favourite landing places in Sussex were Hastings, Bexhill and Eastbourne. Mary Waugh, in her classic study *Smuggling in Kent and Sussex* suggests that the most 'notorious' landing place in Sussex for smuggled goods was Bulverhythe and that 'these smuggling beaches were well served by a network of roads which ran back along sandstone ridges towards the gang headquarters inland.'

Horace Walpole travelled with his friend Mr Chute of Vine to 'the wretched village of Robertsbridge', but there was only one bed available as all the rest were occupied by smugglers, with whom it was suggested one of them should share a bed. So they travelled on to Battle, to 'a still worse inn, crammed with excise officers, one of whom had just shot a smuggler'.

Thomas Turner mentions in his diary: 'Nov. 24, 1763—Mr Banister, having lately taken from the smugglers a freight of brandy, entertained Mr Carman, Mr Fuller, and myself, in the even, with a bowl of punch'.

The smugglers' ships were often cutters, clinker built with a tall mast and a large spread of sail; in the eighteenth century many of these were built at Hastings, until government action drove the building of smuggling ships abroad to France and the Low Countries.

Legendary stories grew up concerning the more notorious smugglers. James Petit or 'Jevington Jig' as he was named after the famous Sussex downland smuggling village, was said to have disguised himself as a woman when the public house he ran was encircled by preventive men. He forgot to take off his large man-sized boots and was spotted. There were also ghost stories, some of which were circulated by the smugglers to keep people away, Arthur Beckett tells of a smuggler's ghost in the Ashdown Forest:

> The forest is haunted by the ghost of a smuggler whose head was shot off in a fight with preventive men. If, perchance, you should happen upon a man without a head, carrying a lantern, the matter is not one that need cause you overmuch fear. For it is merely the ghost of this smuggler seeking the place wherein he laid his kegs of sprits before such time as the King's men did him that ill-service.

Public sympathy was often with individual or small groups of smugglers, but the activities of the notorious smuggling gangs, often organised by shady financiers in London who were never caught, caused some local hostility. There was an early smuggling gang based at Mayfield and smugglers took advantage of the local organisational vacuum at Groombridge, on the Kent–Sussex border, when Groombridge Place was empty between 1730 and 1750, to form the successful, but vicious Groombridge Gang, which terrorised the local inhabitants. It is claimed that the Gang sold 3,000 lb of tea a week, mostly landed in Sussex or Lydd and collected on horseback.

The Groombridge Gang was led by Robert Moreton and John Bowra, son of the local churchwarden. Other members of the gang were known by nicknames, such as 'Flushing Jack', 'Old Joll' and 'Nasty Face'. John Bowra was arrested in 1737, whilst running tea between Eastbourne and Pevensey, but was acquitted at his trial. He later became a successful land surveyor and cartographer. The other members of the gang were arrested in 1749.

Privateering took place off the Sussex coast in the eighteenth century. The nickname of 'chopbacks' given to Hastings fishermen resulted from an incident when a Dutch vessel was boarded by the Ruxley gang in 1768 and the captain murdered by having his spine chopped across the back. There was an earlier local Hastings band of smugglers known as 'The Outlaws' or 'The Transports' in the 1720s and 1730s.

Arthur Beckett knew one of the Alfriston Gang of smugglers in old age, who told him how a revenue officer's horse reins were cut to prevent his pursuit. Beckett comments:

Alfriston High Street & Star & George Inns, 1891.

A Seizure of Smuggled Goods at Eastbourne Customs House. (*Cart labelled 'Birling'*)

Nearly all the Eastern Downs were the scenes of this Gang's exploits. Jevington has seen them pass on their way from Crowlink Gap; Hindover Barn was one of their storehouses, and neighbouring pig-pounds, furze-bushes, and chalk-pits have sheltered their contraband.

The cliffs between Eastbourne and Seaford were also the scene of much smuggling activity. The actor Charles Dibdin stayed at the Lamb Inn at Eastbourne in 1789 and set out for a moonlight walk towards Brighton with a friend. As they neared Seaford and the moon vanished:

As the sky became more obscure, a proportionally brilliant, but terrific, effect was produced by the sudden glare of innumerable signals of fire along the whole line of coast, proceeding from flash-boxes; and as we passed the end of a gloomy defile, cut in a chalk road in the direction of the sea, we were suddenly met by about two hundred horses ridden or led by perhaps half that number of smugglers, all well armed, and each horse carrying as many casks of 'moonshine' as could be slung on his back. They challenged us with much civility; asked where we were going; and, on being informed, said we must not proceed further in that direction, but accompany them for a few miles, when they would set us down in a place much nearer Brighton than we then were; this arrangement was imparted in a good-natured tone, but yet one of so much decision that we had no alternative but to fall in with their humour. They insisted on our each tasting a glass of god-send, as they chose to christen some excellent brandy.

One of the company was the brother of the landlord of the Lamb Inn, who told Dibden that 'they had made a capital night's work'. They were taken on horseback and 'liberated' after about an hour, being cautioned 'to say nothing about the good company we had been in!'

There is evidence of landings of smuggled goods at Cuckmere Haven, Birling Gap, Smugglers Bottom at Crowlink, Seaford Bay, Saltdean and Rottingdean. The 'Jevington Jiggs' were the major gang here, in the 1780s, with tunnels from The Eight Bells Pub and Filching Manor. An extraordinary newspaper account of 1783 relates the trying of an exciseman by a 'jury' of smugglers:

One night last week Mr Marson, Excise Officer at Newhaven, was seized by six or eight smugglers, who escorted him to their main body, composed of near two hundred, assembled at the seaside, by whom the Excise man was tried for shooting a smuggler some time since, when, happily for him, he was acquitted by a majority of ten and suffered to depart unhurt. This was, indeed, turning the tables. Only try to conceive the state of things when smugglers apprehended and tried for their lives Excise officers.

A diary extract of 1814 about Rottingdean notes:

The village is also noted along the coast for bringing things on shore without paying revenue duties, for which innocent and beneficial practice (sad to relate) Captain Dunk, the Butcher, paid £500 and ten of his worthy friends were lodged in Horsham Jaol or, in their elegant language, were sent for a few months to college to improve their manners.

Smuggling is the chief support of the inhabitants at which they are very dexterous—a great deal being carried on at a Gap called Salt Dean gap about three quarters of a mile East, the goods being hid in the furze about here until they can be conveniently carried away. In which trade the leading man is Captain Dunk the butcher, a well known character along the coast.

A Hastings fisherman told Arthur Beckett:

My father was a wunnerful large smuggler, an' so was my gran'father. Soon after the Battle of Waterloo, my gran'father uster go over in a little packet from Rye to Boulogne and bring back a lot o' lace an' silk. He uster take me with him, an he'd wrap lace round an' round my body, an' sometimes I've had as many as five or six pairs of lady's silk stockings on, one over the other; an' when we got ashore gran'father uster take me upstairs an' undress me.

Brighton and Hove beaches were used for landings, and the smuggled goods often stored in the Lanes in Brighton before being moved inland. Shoreham was used for the illegal export of wool as early as 1274. Further west, Worthing beach was a fertile landing spot, with goods them being moved through the gap in the Downs via Findon and Washington. The involvement of the whole community is revealed by a Hailsham legend of two sisters by the name of Fox who were known locally as 'The Whistling Sisters' because they kept watch and warned the local smuggling gang of danger by means of a shrill whistle.

I have not traced any authentic Sussex smuggler songs, but Rudyard Kipling's poem 'A Smugglers' Song', although written half a century after the demise of smuggling through the advent of free trade, captures the essence of romance and danger, the complicit assent of communities and the type of goods smuggled. It has been set to music in several versions and is a good example of a fairly recent composition entering the folk song repertoire because of its valid description of a tradition and it is often performed:

> 'A Smugglers' Song'
>
> *If you wake at midnight, and hear a horse's feet,*
> *Don't go drawing back the blind, or looking in the street,*

Them that asks no questions isn't told a lie.
Watch the wall. My darling, while the Gentlemen go by!

Chorus: Five-and twenty ponies,
Trotting through the dark—
Brandy for the Parson,
'Baccy for the Clerk;
Laces for a lady; letters for a spy,
And watch the wall, my darling, while the Gentlemen go by!

Running round the woodlump if you chance to find
Little barrels, roped and tarred, all full of brandy-wine;
Don't you shout to come and look, nor take 'em for your play;
Put the brushwood back again,—and they'll be gone next day!

If you see the stable-door setting open wide;
If you see a tired horse lying down inside;
If your mother mends a coat cut about and tore;
If the lining's wet and warm—don't you ask no more!

If you meet King George's men, dressed in blue and red,
You be careful what you say, and mindful what is said.
If they call you 'pretty maid', and chuck you 'neath the chin,
Don't you tell where no one is, nor yet where no-one's been!

Knocks and footsteps round the house—whistles after dark—
You've no call for running out till the house-dogs bark.
Trusty's here, and Pincher's here, and see how dumb they lie—
They don't fret to follow when the Gentlemen go by!

If you do as you've been told, likely there's a chance
You'll be give a dainty doll, all the way from France,
With a cap of Valenciennes, and a velvet hood—
A present from the Gentlemen, along o' being good!

A number of false ghost stories were either deliberately put about by smugglers to discourage access to certain sites, or because of misinterpretation of the night time activities of smugglers; an example is the following episode at Edburton:

One morning the whole place was in consternation, owing to a report that two men had been frightened close to a large wood by a ghost, which appeared in the shape of an animal about the size of a calf, with two flaming eyes. Everyone was afraid to go near the place. Mr Thomas Marshall... went and examined it, and found a large quantity of smuggled goods.

12

Songs of the People

In 1752, John Burton described the 'sharp pitch' and 'goatish noise' of Sussex traditional singers and in 1861 Mark Antony Lower commented on *The Sussex Whistling Song* (*The Devil & the Sussex Farmer's Wife*): 'The effect, when continued by strong whistles of a group of lusty countrymen, is very striking, and cannot be adequately conveyed by description'.

But by the end of the nineteenth century, it was realised that a superb set of songs was ripe for collection and a fine harvest was gathered in by expert collectors from talented singers. The county is particularly rich in magnificent pastoral songs with haunting and evocative melodies.

Sussex Folksong Collectors and Their Singers

John Broadwood, the vicar of Lyne and uncle of the famous collector Lucy Broadwood privately published the first collection of Sussex folk songs, entitled *Old English Songs from the Weald of Surrey and Sussex in 1843*. John Broadwood describes his collection of songs as 'sung by the Peasantry' of the Surrey and Sussex Weald and as 'collected by one who has learnt them by hearing them sung every Christmas from early childhood by the country people who go about the Neighbouring Houses singing, 'wassailing' as it is called at that season.' His purpose was:

> to rescue them from oblivion and to afford a specimen of genuine Old English Melody … the airs are set to music exactly as they are now sung, to resave them from oblivion and to afford a specimen of genuine old English melody. [The words are] given in their original rough state with an occasional slight alteration to render the sense intelligible.

This is recognised as the first set of English folk songs featuring words and music collected together, the music being arrangements by W. A. Dusart, an organist from Worthing. Margaret Dean-Smith, formerly Librarian to The English Folk Dance and Song Society commented that the collection is 'the first to be made of folksong airs for their own sake'. A revised edition came out in 1890, with new arrangements by Lucy Broadwood's cousin Herbert Birch Reynardson under the title of *Sussex Songs*, which also contained 16 songs attributed to Lucy, at least one of which was collected by her father Henry.

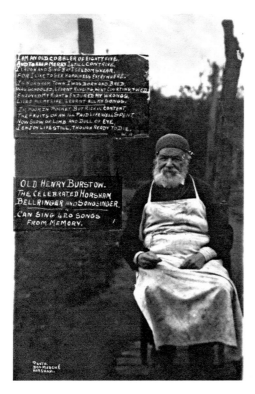

Henry Burstow—Horsham Folk Singer, Bell Ringer and Cobbler.

John's niece, Lucy, lived at Horsham and was the honorary secretary and later president of the Folk Song Society, founded 1898, and editor of its academic journal. Her substantial collecting is featured in *English County Songs* (1893)—of which Ralph Vaughan Williams said 'This may be said to be the starting point of the modern folk song movement'. In her foreword Lucy says:

> The following songs, noted chiefly in Sussex and Surrey since 1892, form only a small part of a very much larger collection made by myself in various counties ... Mr Henry Burstow, to whom I am indebted for most of the Sussex songs here given, was sixty-eight years old in 1893 when he sang them to me. He is a native of Horsham, which up to the year 1893 he had 'never left for a night, except once for a week'. Mr Burstow is well known in Sussex and parts of Surrey as a bell-ringer, and he is also in great request as a singer. He is proud of knowing 400 songs, and keeps a valuable list of their titles, of which he allowed me to make a copy. He once, by request, sang all his songs to a gentleman; 'it took a month to do it!' Many of the songs on Mr Burstow's list, which by their titles promised to be amongst the very oldest ballads, were considered by him to be unfit for ladies' ears, and, as he could not detach the tunes from the words, the airs unfortunately remain un-noted.

One of these was *Salisbury Plain*, which concerns casual sex and highway robbery, but is a rather moving song featured in the *Penguin Book of English Folk Songs* and beautifully recorded by the Sussex singer Shirley Collins.

Mr Burstow learnt very many 'old songs and ballets (sic) off shoemakers who were always singing at their work.' Others he learnt from labourers who often could not read. Some songs he learnt from his father and mother.

Lucy Broadwood's large collection of diaries give fascinating details of her song collecting; for example, in 1881, she paid S. Willett of Cuckfield for several songs, including 'Twankydillo'. Direct payment to singers by collectors is I think quite unusual.

Kate Lee, who studied at both the Royal Academy of Music and the Royal College of Music and was a professional singer, was the first secretary of the Folk Song Society and she collected about 50 songs from James and Thomas Copper of Rottingdean, as recounted in her article 'Some Experiences of a Folk Song Collector':

> Last and not least I come to my collection of Sussex Songs, all found in the little village of Rottingdean, near to fashionable Brighton. I shall never forget the delight of hearing the two Coppers, who gave me the songs, and who are now members of the Society. Mr William [*sic*] is a foreman of a farm, and his brother is the landlord of the 'Plough Inn' [*sic*], a very small public-house. They were so proud of their Sussex songs, and sang them with an enthusiasm grand to hear, and when I questioned them as to how many they thought they could sing, they said they thought about 'half a hundred.' You had only to start either of them on the subject of the song and they commenced at once. 'Oh, Mr Copper, can you sing me a love song, a sea song, or a plough songs? It did not matter what it was, they looked at each othe significantly, and with perfectly grave faces off they would go. Mr Thomas Copper's voice was as flexible as a bird's. He always sang the under part of the song like a sort of obbligato, impossible, at first hearing, to put down ... I simply tired out the two Mr Coppers after three evenings' hard work.

The songs noted by Kate Lee included *The Lark in the Morning*. She mistakenly called James Copper 'William', and got the wrong public house for Tommy (he was landlord of the Black Horse, a fine old pub still surviving under its correct name in the High Street). James Copper wrote 28 of the family songs down in 1922, and his son Jim produced a larger book collection in 1936. James had been a carter and then the farm bailiff to William Brown, a substantial Rottingdean farmer and his grandson Bob remembered him in retirement and helping with rookscaring and singing *Two Old Crows*, which Bob kindly taught to me. Another of James's favourites was *Admiral Benbow*. Tom was a shepherd before becoming the landlord of the Black Horse.

Unique elements about the Copper family tradition, which has continued for many generations, are the family collection of songs (though several share a common Sussex heritage with other singers) and the harmony singing, which James's grandson Bob thought ultimately came from church singing. Bob Copper carried on the family tradition, singing with his cousin Ron and later with his son John, and daughter Jill and their partners. The Coppers have been extensively recorded and collected and have formed a vital element in the Second Folk Revival of the 1950s onwards. Yet another generation of Coppers, 'The Young Coppers' is now appearing at folk clubs and festivals and have produced a CD, with a title of typical Copper/Sussex humour *Passing Out*.

The Northern collector Anne Gilchrist collected some Sussex songs at the turn of the nineteenth and twentieth centuries whilst staying with her brother at Blackham, including

Some Tyrant Has Stolen my True Love Away. Percy Merrick collected many songs from the Sussex farmer Henry Hills of Lodsworth and in 1901 he contributed 52 of *these songs to the Journal of the Folk-Song Society. These included the beautiful pastoral song Searching for Lambs*, and *The Farmer's Glory, John Barleycorn, The Fisherman, Bold General Wolfe, The Golden Vanity, Low Down in the Broom, I'm Seventeen Come Sunday, Sheepcrook and Black Dog* and *Young Edwin in the Lowlands Low*.

Henry Hills's repertoire was magnificent. Percy Merrick wrote of him:

Mr Hills is now about 68 years of age. He was born at Lodsworth, a village lying between Midhurst and Petworth, in Sussex, of which place both his parents were natives, and where his father had a large farm for many years. Here he spent the first thirty years of his life, and it was mostly from the inhabitants of this neighbourhood that he acquired his rather large repertoire of upwards of sixty ditties. In 1863, after the death of his father, he took a farm on Black Down ... and after remaining there for about fifteen years he occupied various other farms in Sussex and Surrey, until in the beginning of 1899 he came to live at Shepperton when I first made his acquaintance.

'Whoever would have thought my old songs could have been any good!', he has said to me. 'When I lived down at Lodsworth I knew lots and lots of them, but I have forgotten a great many of them now ... The Carters used to be always at it when they were along with their horses ... Just take up a stone and rattle it on the handle of the plough and sing to them, and the horses would go along as pretty and well as possible ... We used to have a carter-chap living in the house, and he could sing scores of songs; sometimes of an evening we would sit up and sing for ever so long—first one would get hold of a ballad, and so on ... I used to hear a lot of songs, too, at harvest-homes, tithe-feasts, rent-dinners, rabbit-hunts, and one place and another. Some of the farmers and men about there could sing out-and-out well-capital, they could.

The greatest of all the folk song arrangers, Ralph Vaughan Williams started collecting in 1903 and collected over 800 tunes (including variants). In May 1904 he collected a number of songs from Harriet Verrall of Monks Gate, including: *Our Captain Cried All Hands, Fare Thee Well my Dearest Dear, Salisbury Plain* and the magnificent and mysterious *A Blacksmith Courted Me*, which exists in several variants and tunes in Sussex and arranged by George Butterworth in his *Folksongs of Sussex* (1912):

A Blacksmith courted me, nine months and better.
He fairly won my heart, wrote me a letter.
With his hammer in his hand he looked so clever,
And if I were with my love I'd live forever.

A Blacksmith courted me, I loved him dearly,
He played upon his pipes both neat and trimly.
With his hammer in his hand he strikes so steady,
He makes the sparks to fly all around his smithy.

I love to watch my love with his hammer swinging,
I love to hear it fall on the anvil ringing.

The note is loud and clear, the sparks are flying,
My love is handsome then, there's no denying.

Oh where has my love gone, with his cheeks like roses?
He's gone across the sea, gathering primroses.
I'm afraid the shining sun might scorch his beauty,
And if I were with my love I'd do love's duty.

Strange news is come to town, strange news is carried,
Strange news flies up and down that my love is married.
Well I wish him joy, though he's my love no longer,
And yet I love him still, my blacksmith yonder.

What did you promise me, when you lay beside me?
You said you'd marry me and not deny me.
It's witness have I none but God Almighty,
And may he reward you well, for slighting of me.

Vaughan Williams collected three songs from Ted Baines, a 70-year-old cowkeeper at Plummers Plain on 22 December 1904, including the moving lament of a wife whose husband has been pressed ganged *All Things Are Quite Silent*. He also collected *Horn Fair* from Frederick Teal at the Wheatsheaf Inn, Kingsfold, and *The Basket of Eggs* and *The Devil and the Ploughman* from Henry Burstow of Horsham. Vaughan Williams seems to be the first Sussex collector to use a phonograph, recording *The Trees They Do Grow High* from David Penfold, the landlord of the Plough Inn at Rusper.

George Butterworth, who tragically died in the First World War, published *Folk Songs from Sussex* in 1912, including *The Ship in Distress* from Mr Harwood of Watersfield and *True Love's Farewell*.

Dorothy Marshall and Clive Carey collaborated in the collection, editing and publication of 228 songs, 15 dances with tunes and 4 mummers' plays, mostly from in or near Chithurst, where Dorothy, from a wealthy background, lived in Chithurst House. Dorothy made the local contacts and did some of the collecting, with Clive making several visits to the village in 1911 and 1912 to be introduced to the singers and collect from them. The singers included the labourer William Lemming, the gardener Frank Albery and Mrs Terry.

Clive Carey was born in Essex and became a chorister at Kings College, Cambridge and a trained singer who studied both piano and composition at the Royal College of Music. He sang folk songs to his own piano accompaniments and arrangements and is first recorded as a member of the Folk Song Society in 1912, when he was a member of the committee and sang at its AGM. Clive and Mary collected *The Soldier and His True Love*, which was sung by the Chithurst Tipteerers on their entry, before the beginning of the play, from F. Dawtrey and Walter Brown at Crowshole in 1911. And *The Moon Shone Bright* from F. Albery at Borden Wood in 1911, this song being sung by the Chithurst Tipteerers at the end of their play. And three carols came from the Compton Tipteerers—*When Righteous Joseph*, *I Saw Three Ships* and *Brave Joseph and Mary*, all collected in the years 1911-12. Inevitably, with his higher profile, fame and contacts, Clive got most of the credit, though he did his best to accredit Dorothy. She sadly died young, but is now receiving more credit from the folksong establishment.

As well as being a fine singer and writer on Sussex life, Bob Copper was also employed as a collector of folk songs in Sussex and Hampshire by the BBC. Fine examples of his collecting is Ned Adams of Hastings, *The Bold Princess Royal*, 1954 and Gladys Stone's *Her Servant Man* (also known as *The Iron Door*. Many of Bob's collected songs are featured in his book *Songs and Southern Breezes*. Bob wrote several excellent books on Sussex traditional life and took part in several radio broadcasts. His first book, the best-selling *A Song for Every Season* (1971) sets the Copper songs in their contexts of traditional, seasonal Sussex farming life, bringing the richness of that life to a whole new generation.

In more recent years, at the end of the twentieth century, Ken Stubbs did a great deal of valuable recording in Sussex, particularly of George Maynard of Copthorne. George 'Pop' Maynard (1872-1962) lived for most of his life in Copthorne, on the boundary of Sussex and Surrey, but worked extensively in Sussex, Surrey and Kent, woodcutting, harvesting and hopping and as a skilled wheelwright. He sang regularly at The Cherry Tree Inn at Copthorne, where his chair was still preserved the last time I was there. Singing was part of the family life; his cousins were well-known singers and he learnt many of his songs from his father, brothers and sisters. George also drew on ballad sheets sold locally and hand-written texts. Ken collected 65 of his songs and wrote two books about him, featuring his songs. Pop's repertoire included: *A Wager*, *The Young and Single Sailor*, *The Banks of the Sweet Primroses*, *The Birds in the Spring*, *The Seeds of Love*, *Polly on the Shore*, *The Irish Hop Pole Puller* and a number of poaching songs including *William Taylor*. His long-playing record, *Ye Subjects of England* (Topic 12T286) includes notes by Ken Stubbs and song notes by Mike Yates. Ken Stubbs wrote:

> All manner of agricultural labour was undertaken by George; harvesting (by hand), hedging and ditching, hop-picking, woodcutting and flawing; supplemented by poaching rabbits and pheasants in hard times. Happily married & took his wife Polly and children hop picking. Four sons and two daughters, his wife died early. I recorded 65 songs from him, some being fragments; I wished later that I had taken down all his music-hall songs. His team won the marbles championship at Tinsley Green in 1948 and he was interviewed on radio and appeared on TV playing marbles.

Ken Stubbs also collected many songs from other Sussex singers in the 1950s and 1960s, including Harry Holman of Copthorne (including *The Life of a Man*); Fanny Pronger of East Grinstead; Ursula Ridley of West Hoathly (including the famous *The Iron Door*), Louey Saunders of Newchapel; George Spicer of Selsfield; Henry Steele of Balcombe; George Townshend of Lewes; 10 from Harry Upton of Balcombe (including *Canadee-i-o*); Jim (Brick) Harber of Three Bridges; Noah Willett of Chelwood Gate (including *While Gamekeepers Lie Sleeping*).

Mike Yates collected many songs from Harry Upton of Balcombe, a shepherd, carter and tractor driver born in 1900, who learnt some of his songs from his parents and performed at shepherding events and at the local Working Men's Club, and featured on the DVD *Why Can't It Always Be Saturday?* Mike Yates has also collected many traveller songs in the south east, including Sussex, featured on his long-playing records, which include Mary Anne Haynes singing *Lady Isabel and the Elf Knight*, the Haynes Family, and Louise Fuller.

Michael Blann (1843-1934) was born in Upper Beeding and started work as a shepherd boy and then shepherd. His uncles were fine singers and he built up a repertoire of songs from places such as Findon Sheep Fair, and wrote them in a book which survives in Worthing Library. He sang at events such as Harvest Suppers and also played the whistle and the jew's harp. In later life he moved to Patching. Michael's book, well published and edited by Colin Andrews, lists about 50 songs and gives full text for about 20, including Sussex favourites such as *The Farmer's Boy*, *Dame Durden* and *The Trees Are All Bare*.

George Attrill was a road mender from Stopham, who was involved in singing sessions at The Swan Inn Fittleworth in his younger days, where he learnt many of his songs and he later played an important part in the Second Folk Revival of the 1960s and 1970s. George remembered a ballad singer visiting Fittleworth every few weeks and standing outside the Swan selling ballad sheets for a penny and tuppence and singing the songs to advertise them.

George Belton helped to manage a small farm in the village of Madehurst, near Arundel. He was born in Oxted in 1898 and worked with horses on many farms in Sussex and Surrey. He was a regular member of the Horsham Songswappers Club for many years. His songs included: *Young Sailor Cut Down in his Prime*, *Green Broom*, *The Bold Fisherman*, *Barbara Allan*, *The Dark Eyed Sailor*, *Jim the Carter Lad* and *All Jolly Fellows that Follow the Plough*.

Female singers include Gladys Stone; Ursula Ridley, a landlady from West Hoathly who learnt most of her songs from an old carter who drove her to and from her boarding school in the First World War. Ken Stubbs, who collected many of her songs explained that the source is the reason why Ursula knew songs not 'fitting' for a young lady to hear. And Clare Clayton of Hassocks who sang *The Six Dukes* and, of course, Shirley Collins.

Sussex also played a very important part in The Second Folk Revival in the 1960s and 1970s. I started going to folk clubs in the Brighton area in the mid 1960s and there were very good clubs booking largely traditional singing guests from all over the British Isles and America on Friday and Sunday in Brighton and at Lewes on Saturdays. Vic and Tina Smith took over the Lewes Arms club in the late sixties and it became one of the best in the country, with a high standard and in fostering the excellent local Sussex traditional singers such as Shirley Collins, the Copper Family and Bob Lewis and in encouraging new talent. Later Vic and Tina moved to the Royal Oak and developed more of a concert style of club and Valmai Goodyear started another folk club at the Lewes Arms in 1987, which moved to The Elephant and Castle and is still going strong. It features traditional music of the British Isles and also has workshops and tune practice sessions, with the publication of two tune books. Will Duke has done much to foster Sussex traditional music with his research and playing of tunes by Scan Tester, who ran a Sussex folk dance band between the wars and whom I saw do a booking at Lewes in the 1970s. Will plays Scan's concertina and has also become a fine singer of mainly Sussex songs.

13

Sussex Worthies, Eccentrics, and Superstitions

Jack Fuller

Mad Jack Fuller, of Brightling Park, was a larger than life figure, a 20-stone MP who organised relief in the Brightling area through the construction of pyramids, obelisks and mock temples, such as Brightling Needle, an obelisk on Brightling Down, a pyramid, a circular temple on Rose Hill and his mausoleum in Brightling churchyard. His family fortune came from the Wealden iron industry and manufacture of guns, and he owned slave plantations in Jamaica. But he generously supported the Arts, including being a patron of Turner, he endowed two professorships, gave bells and a barrel organ to Brightling Church. He died in 1834 and according to legend is buried in his mausoleum sitting upright, with a bottle of claret on a table in front of him.

The Miller's Tomb, Highdown

The Miller's Tomb, on Highdown Hill above Salvington, was built by an eighteenth-century miller, John Olliver; he used to visit his tomb daily to meditate, though it was rumoured that he was a smuggler using the site as a lookout and his mill as a means of signalling. Olliver died in 1793, aged 84 and is said to be buried upside down in the tomb, because he thought that Judgement Day would turn the world topsy turvey and that he would be the only man the right way up. Olliver carefully planned his funeral; all the mourners were instructed to wear bright clothing and the burial service was to be read by a young girl. There is a tradition that if you run round the tomb seven times, Olliver's ghost will come out and chase you.

Phoebe Hessel

Phoebe's gravestone is in St Nicholas churchyard, Brighton, prominent besides the main broad path and has inscribed on it:

Above left: The Miller's Tomb at Highdown.

Above right: Phoebe Hessel's Grave, St Nicholas Church Brighton, 2003. (*Geoff Doel*)

In memory of Phoebe Hessel who was born in Stepney in the year 1713. She served for many years as a private soldier in the 5th Regiment of foot in many parts of Europe and in the year 1745 fought under the command of the Duke of Cumberland at the Battle of Fontenoy, where she received a bayonet wound in her arm. Her long life commenced in the time of Queen Anne, extended to the reign of George IV by whose munificence she received comfort and support in her later years. She died in Brighton where she had long resided. December 12th 1821. Aged 108 years.

Phoebe disguised herself as a man and enlisted as a soldier to follow her sweetheart, Samuel into the army. Both of them were wounded in action, and when Samuel was invalided back to England, Phoebe revealed her sex to the wife of her general. She was married to Samuel for 20 years and after his death married William Hessel, who may have been a Brighton fisherman. There are a number of folk songs of the period involving young ladies joining the army in disguise, which may have been influenced by this real-life occurrence.

Phoebe kept a stall near the Steine in Brighton for several years, selling apples, bull's eyes and gingerbread. She was distinctive in wearing a black poke bonnet and black cloth coat over a white apron, and a pair of man's boots. She also sold fish and other items in surrounding villages by donkey. After William's death Phoebe spent some time in the poorhouse, but discharged herself at the age of 93, being allowed two pairs of stockings on her departure according to the records. A Brighton historian met her at this time and records her wearing a brown serge dress, a clean white apron, a black cloth cloak surmounted by a red handkerchief spotted white and an antique bonnet over a mob cap. She liked to show her bayonet scar.

At the celebrations to mark the fall of Napoleon in 1814, Phoebe sat next to the vicar of St Nicholas's church as Brighton's oldest inhabitant, then aged 101, sat beside the vicar of Brighton. She was also present at the coronation celebrations of George IV. The Prince Regent had allowed her a pension of £18 a year, and called her 'a jolly old fellow.'

In 1792 Phoebe was responsible for bringing to justice mail robbers and murderers who struck at Goldstone Bottom (where they were later hanged) and were detected at the Red Lion at Shoreham. The story features in Tennyson's poem *Rizpath*.

Samuel Johnson

A famous eccentric who frequently visited Brighton—Dr Samuel Johnson—commented that the place (pre-Regency of course) was 'so truly desolate that if one had a mind to hang one's self for desperation at being obliged to live there, It would be difficult to find a tree on which to fasten the rope.'

The Prince Regent/George IV

George was a controversial figure, though very popular in Brighton. He once drove a carriage down the steep and narrow Keere Street in Lewes for a wager. According to E. V. Lucas the Burwash bell ringers refused to ring the bells when he passed through the village, because no provision had been made for their beer! On one occasion he spotted his 'dipper', Martha Gunn, put some butter into her apron pocket in the Royal Pavilion kitchen. He engaged her in conversation and edged her near the fire so that the butter melted all over her. He laughed, but compensated her with ten shillings.

Rudyard Kipling

When Rudyard Kipling lived in Rottingdean the landlord of the White Horse oganised horse-drawn coach excursions from Brighton to see the outside of Kipling's house 'The Elms'. One of these excursions damaged Kipling's wall and he wrote to the landlord of the pub complaining. He received no answer and tried again to no effect. He called in at the pub to ask why and was told by the landlord that he hoped he would send further letters as he was selling them for two shillings and sixpence each! Kipling fortunately saw the funny side of this.

John Ruskin

Ruskin was very fond of Fulking and particulary enjoyed the fine sunsets over the Downs. Fulking is on the spring line between the porous chalk and the impervious clay and is a good place for natural springs. A local story tells, rather strangely, that the inhabitants asked Ruskin's advice as to how to harness the water and the result was the erection of a fountain in his honour in 1886 'To the glory of God and in honour of John Ruskin'. Palm XXVIII is quoted on the structure: 'That they might see their hope in God and not forget but keep his Commandments who brought steams also out of the Rock'.

The spring clearly preceded this as it was a popular location for sheep washing.

Above left: Keere Street, 2010. (*Geoff Doel*)

Above right: Ruskin's Spring and Fountain, Fulking. (*Victorian Web*)

Virginia Woolf

She purchased The Round House in Pipe Passage, Lewes, the base of which was erected as a windmill in 1802: 'We've bought a house in Lewes, on the spur of the moment. It's the butt end of an old windmill, so that all the rooms are either completely round or semi-circular'.

But she and her husband never lived there and soon sold it.

Eccentricities at Uppark

Sir Harry Featherstonehaugh was the owner of the splendid mansion of Uppark on the South Downs above Harting. He had a somewhat wild youth and Emma (later Hamilton and mistress of Nelson) was his mistress and is said to have danced naked on one of the tables; a visiting doctor suggested that to see this is would be a cure for impotency! When she was distressed financially and abandoned by society after the death of Nelson, Sir Harry sent her a large sum of money, despite being heavily in debt himself.

Sir Harry in old age caused a local sensation by marrying his dairymaid, Mary Ann Bullock. The span of Sir Harry's life combined with that of his wife (died 1875) and his sister-in-law (Frances, who inherited, died 1895) covered 141 years. H. G. Wells' mother became Miss Bullock's maid in 1850 and commented in her diary that at Christmas 'Up Park just did nothing but eat.' Wells' father became a gardener there in 1851 and the future Mrs Wells left to get married. H. G. Wells descibed Uppark as 'a handsome great house looking south-ward, with beechwoods and bracken thickets to shelter the dappled deer of its wide

Uppark, 1998. (*Geoff Doel*)

undulating downland park.' When Frances Bullock inherited Uppark she employed H. G. Wells's mother to be housekeeper. H. G. Wells wrote in his *Experiment in Autobiography*:

> My mother became housekeeper at Uppark in 1880 ... Except that she was thoroughly honest, my mother was perhaps the worst housekeeper that was ever thought of. She had never had the slightest experience in housekeeping. She did not know how to plan work, control servants, buy stores or economize in any way. She did not know clearly what was wanted upstairs. She could not even add up her accounts with assurance and kept them for me to do for her.
>
> ... during her thirteen years' sway at Up Park and thanks largely to the reliefs and opportunities that came to me through that brief interval of good fortune in her life, I had been able to do all sorts of things.

Frances took a Miss Sutherland to be her companion and Wells comments:

> The place had a great effect on me; it retained a vitality that altogether overshadowed the ebbing tide of upstairs life, the two elderly ladies in the parlour following their shrunken routines.

Wells lived at Uppark in 1880/1 and at Christmas got snowed in and put on theatricals and wrote a newspaper:

A great snow storm snowed me up for nearly a fortnight and I produced a daily newspaper of a facetious character—'The Up Park Alarmist'—on what was properly kitchen paper—and gave a shadow play to the maids and others, in a miniature theatre I made in the Housekeeper's room.

Wells frequently stayed there and the ventilation shafts and upstairs and below-ground servants' rooms and tunnels inspired the respective locations of the Eloi and the Morlocks in *The Time Machine*.

Marriage and Courtship Customs

When a Sussex miller's son was married, they locked the mills sweeps into the position called 'miller's glory' during the church ceremony, to bring good luck. This consisted of two sweeps being vertical and the other two horizontal, to form a cross. Sussex marriages often featured a 'bride pie', with a thick crust, and a hen full of eggs in the middle as an emblem of fertility. This is featured in the song 'Arthur of Bradley':

> *And then they did foot it, and toss it,*
> *Till the Cook had brought up the Posset,*
> *The Bride-pye was brought forth,*
> *A thing of mickle worth,*
> *And so all, at the Bed-side,*
> *Took leave of Arthur and his Bride.*

Superstitions

Charlotte Latham claims:

Many of our Sussex superstitions are probably of Saxon origin, amongst which may be the custom of bowing or curtseying to the new moon or Lady Moon, as she is styled, to deprecate bad luck.

Beware, too, of singing before breakfast: if you sing before breakfast, you will cry before night.

It is ominous of evil to spill salt, or to lay your knife and fork across each other.

Green is an unlucky colour. I have known several instances of mothers absolutely forbidding it in articles of dress, or in the furniture of their houses.

Let not Friday be your wedding day, or you and your wife will lead a cat-and-dog life.

Begin not a piece of work on Friday or you will never finish it, neither must you set off on a journey, nor put out to sea on a Friday, or some misfortune will befall you. The superstitious dread of placing any dependence on this day is almost universal. A tradition, I have heard, that Adam and Eve ate the forbidden fruit upon a Friday, assigns a very early origin to its unfortunate reputation.

I have often heard our cook repeating over her churn, when the butter was slow in forming:

Come, butter, come,
Come, butter, come,
Peter stands at the gate,
Waiting for a buttered cake,
Come, butter, come!

And this charm she repeated three times, in order that it might oblige the witch, who had affected the cream, and, like Robin Goodfellow, 'bootless made the breathless housewife churn', to run away, and at the same time bring the good fairies to her assistance.

The apple charm is very simple, consisting merely in every person present fastening an apple on a string, hung and twirled round before a hot fire. The owner of the apple that first falls off is declared to be upon the point of marriage; and as they fall successively, the order in which the rest of the party will attain to matrimonial honours is clearly indicated; single blessedness being the lot of the one whose apple is the last to drop.

A bride, on her return from church, is often robbed of all the pins about her dress by the single women present, from the belief that whoever possesses one of them will be married in the course of the year.

Andrew Allen, in his *Dictionary of Sussex Folk Medicine* draws attention to the amazing medical lore in the 'Cowfold Churchwardens' Accounts' for the reign of Edward IV, including advice not to bathe in May, but to eat figs and raisins and drink 'swete' drinks. His book also lists some extraordinary folk cures, including eating oysters lightly fried in bacon fat for flu (at Selsey) and this one for ague: 'Take a Spyder alive, cover it with new soft crummy Bread without bruising it; let the Patient swallow it fasting.'

Lewes experienced a plague of Frogs—Frog Lane commemorates this. Amberley has a propensity to flooding and the Amberley women are supposed to be born with webbed feet! They were also called 'yellow bellies' because of lifting their skirts to warm themselves over smoky fires.

14

Witchcraft and
Anti-Social Behaviour

Witchcraft

There is only one recorded hanging of a witch in Sussex—Margaret Cooper at Horsham in 1574. Horsham was also the site of the last recorded witchcraft trial in the county, in which Alice Nash was accused of bewitching a little girl, Elizabeth Slater, who later died; she was found not guilty and released. Judy Middleton, in her *A History of Hove* mentions accusations at Lewes in 1588 that were dropped and also gives some helpful statistics setting Sussex indictments for witchcraft in context:

> Margery Banger, a widow, and her daughter Joane, were thought to be witches. In the Acts Books of the Archdeaconry Court at Lewes in May 1588 they were cited as 'vehemently suspected to be notorious witches.' Fortunately for them, four women came forward less than a month later to act as compurgators and the accusation was dropped. Compurgation under old English law was the clearing of the accused by witnesses who testified as to their innocence. Although the years 1588-97 recorded the highest number of indictments for witchcraft in the home circuit, Sussex as a whole did not follow the general fashion of witch-hunting, in comparison to other counties. During the years 1558-1736 only 17 people were indicted for witchcraft at the assizes.

There is much folklore about the bewitching of animals. Charlotte Latham records the tradition of hag riding (witches riding and tiring out horses at night) in Sussex:

> Not many years ago a farmer residing on the western border of Sussex and Surrey seriously declared that the witches were in the habit of riding his horses by night, and they were often found by him in the morning covered with dirt and perspiration, and in a state of great exhaustion. This marvel, too, like many of our ghost stories, might probably be accounted for by the lawless practices of the gangs of smugglers, who took the liberty of borrowing the farmer's horses for the night-work of bringing up their kegs of brandy from the coast.

Dame Prettylegs of Albourne was thought to be a witch linked to horses, also with a smuggling link. Tony Wales in his *West Sussex Village Book* writes:

As in many Sussex villages, Albourne once had its own witch. Her name was Dame Prettylegs, and she was much addicted to placing spells on horses. The fact that her husband was known as a smuggler may have had something to do with the reputation which she cultivated.

According to legend, Hannah Clarke, a Hastings witch, was employed to keep a look out for attacking French ships in the middle ages, using her broomstick and accompanied by her two cats. She and her cats used to sleep in front of the fire at the Stag Inn until her broomstick was stolen and she left in quest of a new one. The bricked-up cats' skeletons found at the pub are supposed to be those of her cats. A ladies' morris team in Hastings is called 'Hannah's Cats'.

In the 1570s two Sussex women, Joan Usbarne of Hailsham and Alice Casselowe of Mayfield were convicted of bewitching bulls.

Wise Women, White Witches and Conjurors

One of the greatest services a white witch or conjuror could render to their communities was to break a witch's spell. Scratching a witch, or drawing her blood with a pin, needle or knife was thought to be an infallible means of arresting a spell. In 1593 a cunning man from Hastings known as Zacharias was consulted by anxious parents who believed that their sick child had been bewitched by a neighbour, 'Mother' Rogers. Zacharias's advice was unusual in that instead of recommending the usual pin thrust into arm or body, he suggested the 'witch' should have a knife inserted into her buttocks. This is an example of how a community when dealing with such a feared and emotive subject as witchcraft could often take the law into their own hands and adminster rough justice (often miscarriages of justice) without recourse to law. Charlotte Latham knew of a wise woman in Bury:

> There is a strong persuasion that certain persons have a supernatural and mysteriously acquired foreknowledge, and there is, I believe, still living in the parish of Bury a cunning woman, to whom young men and maidens resort, to inquire from her whether their presumptive husbands or wives will be short, or tall, rich or poor, dark or fair, only a few months since I heard of three young girls, attired in their Sunday best, walking from a distant town to consult her.

A scalded woman visited by a wise-woman who 'bowed her head over the wound, crossed two of her fingers over it and repeated words—then breathed on it.

> *There came two Angels from the North,*
> *One was fire, one was Frost.*
> *Out Fire: in Frost,*
> *In the name of the Father, Son and Holy Ghost.*

Highwaymen

Tennyson's poem *Rizpath* uses a real instance of highwaymen in Sussex robbing at Goldstone Bottom. They were detected at the Red Lion, Shoreham, and hanged at the scene of their crimes.

Skimmity Rides and Rough Music

An innkeeper in Thomas Hardy's *The Mayor of Casterbridge* neatly sums up the custom of skimmmity riding: "'tis a old foolish thing they do in these parts, when a man's wife is—well, not too particularly his own' It is the community's way of expressing disapproval by a procession with people dressing up as the characters concerned and accompanied by 'rough music' making a raucous sound. And it happened in Sussex too! John Osborn Greenfield (1812-1869) was familiar with the custom and describes a skimmity ride in detail in his book *Tales of Old Petworth*:

It sometimes happened that a strong-minded, jealous woman beat her husband, and then a 'skimmington' took place, especially if the wife had been guilty of a 'faux pas' with another man. Hogarth has given a most graphic picture of it. A shift was elevated on a pole, crowned with a formidable pair of horns; on an ass the husband and wife were personated by two of the riff-raff of the town, both men, but one of them dressed as a woman, who seated astride on the animal turned herself round to the other, who sat with his face to the donkey's tail, and every now and then struck him with a wooden ladle. The wife generally carried a large iron porridge pot before her ... rough music accompanied them ... We had no police in those days, and the rabble had their full swing of such sort of amusement.

I remember a famous skimmington on a Whit-Tuesday ... Our brewer and tap-boy were amongst them. The woman was enacted by Charles Herrington, always first in any such affair... The parties dressed at the Angel, and the procession started from that place ... Herrington was nicely dressed, and being young, slightly made, and of a fair complexion and delicate features, he made rather a good-looking woman. The horns worn on the man's forehead were ram's horns, partly silvered and partly gilt. I had them some years in my possession. The parties represented were Jack Nevatt, a footman of the late Lord Egremont's family, and his wife, Nan Nevatt ... a woman of a notoriously bad life and character, both before and after her marriage ... It is scarcely to be credited that Mr W., a man of fifty, with a wife and a family of seven or eight children ..., a man of property, should have 'taken up' with such a strumpet ... The roughs and boys of the town who knew their meeting places, used to watch them, and if he did not fee them well, and often if he did, used to hunt them about and sometimes up to his very door. His wife and daughters as they sat at their windows have often seen him so chased. Once they drove the guilty couple through the thickest hedge on the sheep downs.

Rough Music, as well as being part of the skimmington, was often used separately as a demonstration of transgression outside the transgressor's house to shame him or her. There are three examples from East Lavant between 1869 and 1872—two for men bullying their wives, the other for a woman beating her husband. And the *West Sussex Gazette* of May 1954 has a description of Rough Music at Burpham in the 1890s against men who showed violence to their wives and children. Effigies were sometimes used, and a correspondent recalled the song used:

> *There is a man lives in this place,*
> *He beat his wife—a sad disgrace!*

He beat her black, he beat her blue,
He made her poor bones rattle too.

Now, if this man don't mend his manners,
We'll have to send him to the tanner's;
And if the tanner don't tan him well
We'll nail him on a nail in hell.

And if that nail should chance to crack
He'll fall upon the Devil's back;
And should the Devil chance to run
We'll shoot him with this fiery gun.

There was an example of rough music at Copthorne for child cruelty as late as about 1950.

Wife sales

At a time when divorce was difficult and hugely expensive, the selling of wives in front of witnesses happened frequently in rural areas. Although this archaic practice offends feminists enormously, many of the examples show the consent of the wives and indeed have often taken place because the wife has a new lover, to whom she is sold. This is done to avoid the husband having to continue to maintain his wife and her children by her new lover.

The *Sussex Weekly Advertiser* has several examples. At Ninfield in November 1790 a man sold his wife one evening for a half pint of gin and then bought her back for a higher price! At Lewes in July 1797 a blacksmith sold his wife to one of his journeymen. In Brighton in February 1799 a man called Staines 'sold his wife by private contract, for 5s and eight pots of beer, to one James Marten of the same place', with two married couples witnessing 'the articles of separation and sale'.

Henry Burstow mentions three cases in his *Reminiscences of Horsham*:

I have been told of a woman named Smart, who, about 1820, was sold at Horsham for 3s and 6d. She was bought by a man named Steere, and lived with him at Billingshurst … Stere … sold her to a man named Greenfield.

Again, at the November Fair, 1825, a journeyman blacksmith … exhibited for sale his wife, with a halter round her neck. She was a good-looking woman with three children, and was actually sold for £2. 5s, the purchaser agreeing to take one of the children. This 'deal' gave offence to some who were present, and they reported the case to the magistrate, but the contracting parties, presumably satisfied, quickly disappeared, and I never hear any more about them.

… The last case happened about 1844, when Ann Holland, known as 'pin-toe Nanny' or 'Nanny pin-toe, was sold for £1 10s. Nanny was led into the market place with a halter round her neck. Many people hissed and booed, but the majority took the matter good-humouredly. She was 'knocked down' to a man named Johnson, at Shipley, who sold his watch to buy her … This bargain was celebrated on the spot by the consumption of a lot of beer by Nanny, her new husband, and friends. She lived with Johnson for one year, during which she had one child, then ran away—finally marrying a man named Jim Smith, with whom she apparently lived happy for many years.

At Brighton in 1826 a market inspector levied one shilling on a wife-sale. A magistrate challenged this and the inspector quoted a bye-law which stated 'Any article not enumerated in these bye-laws pays one shilling'. The most recent case might be that at Yapton in 1898, recorded in an editorial note in the *Sussex County Magazine* for 1926:

As late as 1898 the old belief that it was quite legal for a man to sell his wife had not quite died out, for the newspapers of that day reported that at the end of the harvest at Yapton, near Littlehampton, a man 'sold his wife to a stranger for 3s'.

15

The Folklore of Sussex Pubs

The Queensbury Arms, Brighton

The Queensbury Arms, Brighton, near the Metropole Hotel, is also know as 'The Hole in the Wall' as it used to sell from a window direct to fishermen on the beach before the erection of the King's Road along the sea front. My maternal grandfather, George Mitchell, was the licensee in the 1940s and 1950s. Many famous politicians used to drink there during party conferences in preference to the hotel bar. It was also frequented by many actors and actresses and features old playbills on the walls.

Hangleton Manor

Hangleton Manor was mentioned in the Domesday Book, when it was owned by William de Warenne. It was later owned by Sir Philip Sidney and the Sackville family and was a manor farm, the farm lasting until my boyhood in the 1950s, when the area was 'developed' for housing and the manor itself narrowly avoided destruction. The fifteenth century 'Old Manor House', survives as a long low wing adjoining the main sixteenth century building, which has high quality sixteenth century panelling and tiling. There are two traditional female ghosts, one of whom gently pushes people. One of the ghosts is of a serving maid, made pregnant by the lord of the manor, who killed the resultant child. A more recent emergence is a story of a monk who cursed the dovecote because of the pigeon droppings. The building is said to be haunted by pigeons, but there are problems with this 'tradition' since the dovecote is seventeenth century (i.e. after the Reformation) and there are no monastic connections anywhere near the site.

The Black Horse Rottingdean

Rottingdean has both a Black Horse and a White Horse, formerly The King of Prussia, pubs. The Black Horse was once run by Tommy Copper of the famous singing family and is an

Hangleton Manor. (*Geoff Doel, 2018*)

The Black Horse, Rottingdean, 2018. (*Geoff Doel*)

attractive building dating from 1513, which once included a forge and which still boasts a delightful snug. It is thought to have been a meeting place for the Rottingdean smugglers.

The Lamb/The Piltdown Man at Piltdown

I was sorry to see the name of 'The Piltdown Man' changed recently in the village of that name, as it commemorated a famous archaeological forgery in the village when an ass's jawbone was used to simulate an early ancestor of mankind. However the name now in use—'The Lamb' is the original name of the pub.

The Snow Drop Inn, Lewes.

The Snow Drop Inn is built on the site of an avalanche which occurred on Christmas Eve 1836: it was described thus in the *Sussex Weekly Advertiser* of January 1837:

THE AVALANCHE IN THE SOUTH DOWNS

On Christmas Eve in 1836 and following a severe snow storm, an avalanche fell from the edge of the Downs and overwhelmed a row of seven cottages that stood under the Downs in South Street, Lewes. Fifteen people were buried in snow and rubble and of these eight were brought out dead. The victims were William Geer (82), Joseph Wood (16), Mary Taylor (42), Phoebe Barden (45), Maria Bridgeman (31), Mary Bridgman (11), Jane Books (25) and Susan Haywood (30).

Their bodies were laid before the poor house and a committee heard the evidence. A child witness had seen a crack open in the snow ' which continued to grow wider until a large quantity came down with extreme violence and on reaching the houses threw them down immediately'.

One survivor, James Rook, a labourer, had spoken to Mary Taylor and begged her minutes beforehand not to go into her cottage but she 'popped in to get a shawl 'and 'was caught in the street'. Robert Hyam landlord of the 'Schooner' whose beer shop faced the line of houses that were destroyed, had warned several inhabitants the night before that a fall was imminent and only and four minutes before the fall ran 'down the passage' telling the cottagers to leave everything and get out and save themselves. He was actually talking to Mrs Barden and Mrs Bridgman when they were overwhelmed by the snow and tried to help them but had to move back to save his own life. The verdict was 'Accidental Death'. The dead were buried at South Malling and their names recorded on a tablet within the church.

George & Dragon, Dragon's Green

An obelisk in the garden commemorates Walter Rudd, who drowned himself in 1893, aged only 26 after being accused of a minor theft. He was an epileptic albino, ostracized by his neighbours, due to his strange appearance and occasional fits. His parents erected a cross in Shipley churchyard, but both vicar and congregation were outraged by the inscription, which concluded: 'May God forgive those who forgot their duty to him who was just and afflicted.' The vicar had the cross removed, so the parents built their son's memorial in the garden of The George and Dragon.

The Red Lion, Shoreham

The Red Lion pub near the old wooden bridge over the Adur at Old Shoreham, dates back to the sixteenth century. In the winter of 1792 a highwayman called James Rock was arrested there after boasting in the bar of a highway robbery he had participated in at Hove. As Tennyson recounts in his gruesome poem *Rizpah*, after his execution his mother collected his bones and buried them at St Nicholas's Church, a stone's throw from the pub. Tamplins, the famous Brighton Brewers, owned the house in Victorian times, when the famous New Year custom of 'The Bushel' was described by Frederick Sawyer:

Red Lion, Shoreham, 2016. (*Geoff Doel*)

A vessel holding a bushel is decorated with flowers, paper, etc., and filled with beer, from which all comers may drink free. The custom was duly observed on January 1st, 1883. I am told … the custom has been observed for 80 years. A bushel corn measure is used, and, when filled, the beer put in it froths up, and with the green paper, etc., looks like a huge cauliflower. The beer is ladled with a pint mug, and drunk from glasses. There is a regular chairman, and the man who ladles out the beer is called 'the baler', and the latter has the privilege of drinking from the measure itself.

Those who drank the full measure were called 'Bushellers'.

The Black Lion, Brighton

The Black Lion Brewery was established in 1546 by a Flemish protestant immigrant, Deryk Carver, who held religious services using the Bible in the vernacular and became one of 'Bloody Mary's seventeen Lewes martyrs. He was burnt in a beer barrel outside the Crown Inn, Lewes and hurled his protestant bible into the crowd. The brewery had a 54 foot well and was used by various brewers in the nineteenth and twentieth centuries, but was demolished in 1968 at a time when there was much vandalous action by, or allowed by Brighton councils. It was rebuilt as a pub in 1974, using original flints and slates. It is said to be haunted, with beer crates apparently moving themselves and a shadowy figure, who disappears, seen pacing up and down.

The White Hart Hotel, Lewes

This is a coaching inn of Tudor origins. It was owned by the famous chef and recipe publisher William Verall from 1737-1760. Tom Paine organised meetings of the Headstrong Club in the Sheriff Room and the Tudor Room.

Black Lion Brewery, Brighton, early 1900s.

Bibliography

Books

Ainsworth, H., *Ovingdean Grange* (Routledge, 1876)

Allen, A., *A Dictionary of Sussex Folk Medicine* (Countryside Books, 1995)

Andrews, C., *Shepherd of the Downs* (Worthing Museum & Art Gallery, 1979)

Anon, *The Brighton Custumal* (Ms 1580)

Anon, *Juvenile Varieties* (Bruce, early nineteenth century)

Axon, W., *Bygone Sussex* (William Andrew & Co., 1897)

Baldwin, L., and Ridsdale, A., *Annals of Old Rottingdean* (Sussex Notes & Queries, 1933)

Beckett, A., *The Spirit of the Downs* (Methuen, 1909); *The Wonderful Weald* (Mills & Boon, 1911)

Belloc, H., *The Four Men: A Farrago* (1911, OUP 1984)

Blencowe, R. W., *South-Down Shepherds and Their Songs at the Sheepshearing Sussex Archaeological Collections* (1849)

Broadwood, J., *Old English Songs from the Weald of Surrey and Sussex* (Privately printed, 1843)

Broadwood, L., *English County Songs* (Leadenhall, 1893); *English Traditional Songs and Carols* (1908)

Burstow, H., *Reminiscences of Horsham* (Gale, 1911)

Butterworth, G., *Folk Songs from Sussex* (Galliard, 1912)

Candlin, L., *Tales of Old Sussex* (Countryside Books 1985, 2011); *Memories of Old Sussex* (Countryside Books, 1987)

Cook, W. V., *The Story of Sussex* (1919, Neilson Press 2010)

Copper, B., *A Song for Every Season* (Heinemann, 1971); *Early to Rise* (Heinemann, 1976); *Songs and Southern Breezes* (Heinemann, 1973); *Bob Copper's Sussex* (SB Publications, 1997)

Doel, F., and Doel, G., *Christmas Past in Sussex* (History Press, 2005); *Folklore of Kent* (History Press 2003, 2009); *The Hop Bin: An Anthology of Hop Picking in Kent and East Sussex* (History Press, 2014); *Mumming, Howling and Hoodening: Midwinter Rituals in Sussex, Kent and Surrey* (Meresborough Books, 1992)

Doel, F., Doel, G., and Deane, T., *Spring and Summer Customs in Sussex, Kent and Surrey* (Meresborough Books, 1995)

Donnelly, P., *Benefits and Beer* (Harting Old Club, 2000)

Etherington, J., *Lewes Bonfire Night* (SB Publications, 1993, revised 1999); 'The Lewes Bonfire Riots of 1847' in *Sussex History* (Autumn 1978)

Frampton, G., 'Clive Carey, Dorothy Marshall and the West Sussex Tradition' in *English Dance and Song* (September–October 1986)

Goring, J., *Burn Holy Fire: Religion in Lewes since the Reformation* (Lutterworth Press, 2003)

Greenfield, J. O., *Tales of Old Petworth* (Lindow Press, 1987)

Hare, C., *The Secret Shore: Tales of Folklore & Smuggling from Sussex & Hampshire* (The South Downs Society, 2016)

Horsfield, T., *The History and Antiquities of Lewes and its Vicinity* 2 vols. (Baxter, 1824–7); *The History and Antiquities and Topography of the County of Sussex* 2 vols. (Baxter, 1835)

Hutton, R., *Stations of the Sun: A History of the Ritual Year in Britain* (OUP, 1996)

Judge, R., *The Jack-in-the-Green* (Brewer, 1979)

Kipling, R., *Puck of Pook's Hill* (Penguin 1906, 1994); *Rewards and Fairies* (1910, Piccolo, 1975)

Latham, C., *Some West Sussex Superstitions Lingering in 1868* (Folklore Society, 1878)

Lee, K., 'Some Experiences of a Folk-Song Collector' in *Folk Song Society Journal* vol. 1 No. 1 (1899-1904)

Leech, K., *The Hastings Traditional Jack in the Green* (Hastings Borough Council, 2008); 'The Oldest Guy in the World' in *English Dance and Song* Vol. 49 No. 2 (September–October 1987)

Lucas, E. V., *Highways and Byways in Sussex* (1904, CreateSpace, 2018)

McCarthy, S., 'Pop Maynard—Lord of the Ring' in *English Dance and Song* (Spring 1982).

Meade-Fetherstonehaugh, M., and Warner, O., *Uppark and its People* (George Allen and Unwin, 1964)

Macdermott, K. H., *The Church Gallery Minstrels of Old Sussex* (1922, Country Books/Ashbridge Press, 2006)

Middleton, J., *A History of Hove* (Philimore, 1979); *Ancient Hove and Portslade* (Local History Publications, 1984, revised 2007)

Moore, J., *Sussex Legends & Folklore* (James Pike Ltd, 1976)

Parish, W. D., *A Dictionary of Sussex Dialect, 1875* (second edition enlarged by Helena Hall, Gardners Books, 1957)

Payne, S., *A Sussex Christmas* (Alan Sutton, 1990)

Payne, S., and Pailthorpe, R. (eds), *Barclay Wills' The Downland Shepherds* (Alan Sutton, 1989)

Pelling, T., *Tales of Goldstone Bottom* (Pelling, 2017)

Pennington, J., *St Cuthman of Steyning—A Journey Through Time* (Steyning Museum & Friends of St Andrew, 1993)

Phillips, B., 'Discovery of a Tumulus at Hove, near Brighton, Containing an Amber Cup' in *Sussex Archaeological Collections* vol. IX (1848)

Sawyer, F., 'Sussex Folk-Lore and Customs Connected with the Seasons' in *Sussex Archaeological Collections* vol. 33 (1883)

Sharp, R. J., 'Sussex Mummers or Tipteerers' in *Sussex County Magazine* (1931)

Simpson, J., *The Folklore of Sussex* (1973, Tempus 2002); *Sussex Local Legends Folklore*, vol. 84 (autumn 1973)

Stuart, D., *Old Sussex Inns* (Breedon Books, 2005)

Stubbs, K., 'The Life and Songs of George Maynard' in *English Dance and Song* (1963)

Tiddy, R., *The Mummers Play* (OUP, 1923)

Toms, H. S., *The Goldstone, Hove Park* (DCM, 1932, p. 725)

Turner, T., *The Diary of a Georgian Shopkeeper, 1754–1765* (OUP, 1979)

Williams, V., and Lloyd, A. L., *The Penguin Book of English Folksongs* (Penguin, 1959)

Wales, T., *Sussex Customs, Curiosities & Country Lore* (Ensign, 1990); *A Sussex Garland* (Countryside Books, 1979); *A Treasury of Sussex Folklore* (SB Publications, 2000); *We Wunt Be Druv: Songs and Stories from Sussex* (Galliard, EFDSS, 1976); *The West Sussex Village Book* (Countryside Books, 1984); *The East Sussex Village Book* (Countryside Books, 1984)

Waugh, M., *Smuggling in Kent & Sussex 1700–1840* (Countryside Books, 1985)

Westwood, J., and Simpson, J., *The Lore of the Land* (Penguin, 2005)

Wills, B., *Shepherds of Sussex* (Robert Hale, 1972)

Woodford, C., *Portraits of Sussex* (Robert Hale, 1972); *Sussex Ways and Byways* (Crown Books, 1968)

CDs

Copper Family, *Come Write Me Down: Early Recordings of the Copper Family of Rottingdean* (Topic, 2001)

Collins, S., *The Sweet Prime-roses* (Topic, 1995)

Collins, S., and Collins, D., *The Harvest Years* (EMI, 2008)

Duke, W., *Out of the Box* (Country Branch)

Duke, W., and Quinn, D., *Scanned* (Country Branch)

Lewis, B., *The Painful Plough* (Foxide Music, 2003)